AF316638

JOCELYN FAMILY'S RULES

Published by Spines
ISBN: 979-8-89383-340-9

JOCELYN FAMILY'S RULES

Yvette Jocelyn

Contents

Dedication

I dedicate this book to my deceased father, Pierre Jocelyn; he guided, cherished, and wanted the best things in life for me.

I also dedicate this book to my deceased mother, Irene Morin; she was the beacon of hope in my life and the person I am today, including the values I hold in my heart, all thanks to her.

To my dearest daughter Keshia Jocelyn, I dedicate this book to you as well. You have been a sweetheart, and since you were born, you've made my life special in ways that I never thought would be possible. Thank you for always being there for me and helping make this book a glorious reality.

This book is also dedicated to my son Richard G. Jocelyn and my granddaughters Victoria Lynn Jocelyn, Stella Jocelyn, and Ruby Jocelyn.

Sisters are a blessing from God, and Gisele Jocelyn, my sister, has been a blessing to me as well. I dedicate this book to her, too, for she has been the warmth of my days throughout my life.

I would also like to thank my Coach, Emmanuel Delorme, who has shown me constant support and guidance and without whom I would never have been able to be so successful in life.

Finally, all this would not have been possible without the constant support and courage shown to me by my sister in Jesus, my counselor, and my best friend, Solange Beauchamp; I will always be honored to have your companionship.

I love you all; you are my fortune and God's gift to me in this humble life.

Chapter 1
Life in the Countryside of Haiti

"Commit your actions to the Lord, and your plans will succeed." –
Proverbs 16:3

All praise belongs to God, who created and blessed us with life on Earth. We are mere mortals, fragile, weak to our cores, struggling to find peace and satisfaction. That is a lousy way to grasp the bounty of life. We are blessed only if we take a moment to wait and ponder over the countless 'rights' that happen all around us, but horrendously, we continue to focus on the 'wrongs' taking place in our surroundings.

In our search for inner peace, we continue to traverse the world blindfolded, demeaning our existence, and failing miserably at the search for the purpose, the reason, the answer to a single question: Why were we born?

Civilizations of countless fools have perished in search of this trivial question when the answer has always been *right there!* Our beating hearts, our tingling senses, the laughter of children, the shining sun, and the world around us all come together to remind us of God's blessing on us. We who have lived sinful life carry on with our thankless existence. Have we ever stopped to thank God? No, because even a lifetime of gratitude will never be enough.

God does not need our thanks; He is at the top in all his glory. If we acknowledge God's blessings, be thankful to him and obey his commandments, we benefit from it; this is the easiest way to find true peace and the most straightforward way to live. We should live a god-fearing life, and our actions should resonate with the commands and will of God.

As the world around us falls into despair, we should never lose hope, for hope will guide us to the path of God.

Our story begins with the biggest blessing of all, the birth of a daughter. The parents, bless them, cry out in joy as God has not forsaken them, and amidst all the fears of childbirth, they came out happy with a bundle of joy in their arms. This was the birth of Yvette Jocelyn and what follows is her journey through the fiery waters of her existence to adulthood. Her journey revolves around many spheres of mortal existence, from crippling grief to abundant happiness, from the depths of despair to the heights of hope.

Yvette was born into the humble Jocelyn family in Les Cayes, Haiti. Being a member of this family came with perks of its own. Her parents lived a God-fearing life and cherished the many ways God has blessed them throughout their existence. From the moment she opened her eyes to look at her parents' smiling faces, she was showered with immense love; as for them, she was a symbol of hope and grace from God.

Yvette's parents were traditional and valued a life devoid of luxuries and irrelevant wants. They followed the principle that one should be content with what they have, and a thirst for power and material objects will throw them off the right path of God. From a young age, they ingrained this sense of living in her soul. They taught her the act of forgiveness, the principle of sharing and valuing the little blessings around her. In return for her parents' love, she loved them back unconditionally and gave them the proper respect they deserved. A childhood with an upbringing like this will never go astray.

Their relationship had no shackles of secrecy as she was encouraged to share whatever troubled her. They always kept the door of suggestions open for her, which in turn helped their relationship foster one more inclined toward friendship. Even when she committed a mistake, she found a pillar of morality and fortitude in them.. They never raised their hand at her, and at times when she seemed only a bit hesitant to listen to them, they always guided her by telling her about the will of God.

The blessings on Yvette continued as her parents made it their purpose to protect and provide for her. They encouraged her to live a healthy life, free from the mental strains of despair and away from all the junk food kids are found to be eating today.

Yvette has many fond memories of her childhood. It was a tradition to go on vacation every few months in their household. Her parents and siblings always tried their best to make her happy; even today, thinking about it brings tears of joy to her eyes. She enjoyed these trips into nature and valued the family time that came as a bonus. Being a part of the Catholic Church, they celebrated Christmas, Easter, and Good Friday with whole revels. They also observed Lent resonate with the sufferings of the poor. For her, the best day of the year was her birthday. It was celebrated with an afternoon party to which most of the extended family was invited.

Yvette still remembers her first day of school in vague bits and pieces, especially how she felt about the whole ordeal. Her parents enrolled her in a local private catholic school named Catholic School of Sister Ann. She was scared and worried about what will happen to her, but at the same time, she wanted to obey her parents' will and make them proud.

Her conflict within was dumbfounded, as when she started attending school regularly, she began making friends with whom she found solace and ease. Those proved to be pleasant days for Yvette, for God was always in her heart, protecting her and cherishing her happiness.

When we were young, time flew, and soon, Yvette became a teenager, beginning her ascent into the uncharted territory of adulthood. Her parents worked hard and therefore earned well, and the support system she had was the best she could have. Food was always on the table, they had a roof over their heads, and a fine assortment of attires could also be found in their wardrobes. These were one of the best days as they always had whatever they needed or desired. Even with all the necessities of life, they did not thrive in their wealth, as they knew that was not the way of God; instead, they always preferred to help the needy and the destitute whenever possible for them.

Keeping in mind her parents' teachings Yvette always kept the best relationship with the people around her. Among her siblings, things always remained amiable; they loved each other and cherished the time God granted them to spend with each other. They helped one another with schoolwork and also shared their belongings. Relationships like these create bonds that can never be broken. Even the friendships Yvette made were based on the same principle of goodwill and kindness. She influenced her peers, and they, too, adopted the positive outlook she possessed for life. This was the charm of her parents' upbringing. They transmitted their positivity to her, and it reflected in all her actions. She knew she was responsible for spreading the exact word of God, and what better way to do it than embodying his teachings in her daily life? For her being content was how God has taught us to live in this world.

Life was moving fast for Yvette, and soon the time came for her to move out and live in the capital city of Haiti, Port –au- Prince. At that time, she was in her early twenties. It was hi-time to start college and experience life at its optimum. During this time, her abode became her cousin

Gladyse's house. She was her maternal cousin. Gladyse was one of her closest family members who lived in the capital. They were already well acquainted, so surprisingly, this abrupt shift in their life came and passed swimmingly. Gladyse had been looking forward to it for a long time as she cherished spending time with Yvette. She used to support her in all her decisions. They became best friends and helped each other in all times of need. Yvette treasured this friendship as life in the capital would have been complicated without her. The best part about Gladyse was she was almost the age of Yvette, which greatly aligned their interests and beliefs . They used to hang out all the time doing all sorts of fun activities two best friends together would do. She was Yvette's life support as she did everything that helped Yvette feel at home. She was loyal and proved to be a good secret keeper for Yvette.

Life in the capital was tough for Yvette. Everyone was always busy and watching people being so energetic around always made her very anxious. Running her eyes across her surroundings, Yvette used to think everyone had something to do here. More like a purpose. Back home, she used to spend a lot of time bonding with her family, but everyone was always busy here in Port-AU-Prince. The cost of living in the capital was a lot more expensive than what it was back at home. She had to cut back on her personal expenses to accommodate her new lifestyle. The capital was full of grocery stores with unique items she hadn't seen before. Every day she met new people who smiled at her and tried to initiate small talk; as much as she liked it, she disliked it at some point too, and it was hard for her to avoid all this.

Although life in the big city was difficult, Yvette had an experience of her own. Life here offered her many different opportunities. The salaries were high, and so were the job prospects. And then, the cherry on top was the easy commute. Traveling from one place to another wasn't as streneous as it was compared to back home.

Yvette was adjusting well to her new lifestyle, but simultaneously, she missed her life back at home. She was a *'shrubs'* girl. She was used to exploring all the countryside's greenery, which was almost impossible in the capital. She missed her family and friends dearly. She missed her home because she was born there and grew up with those people. She had made many memories there and revered them very much.

The college had been a long time coming for Yvette. She wanted to land a good job, and for that, she needed to have a college degree. She also wanted to connect and study with a diverse population of students because she wanted more life exposure. Her dream came true in Port-au-Prince.

God had blessed Yvette time and time again, which was apparent in her smooth journey. Why was God blessing her at every turn? Because she was a servant of God. Her outlook on life revolved around pleasing God in every move she made. She chose to be polite when she could have screamed. She always spoke the truth even when she could've easily lied. She was humble when she could have been proud. She showed courage and steadfastness while facing every obstacle when most people would've quickly lost hope. She proved herself repeatedly and became an exemplary example for everyone to follow. How she lived life was no ordinary feat; it demanded her to vary Satan's deception tactics and how he lures his prey towards sin, causing them suffering and turmoil with no end. This was God's blessing, as the path she had chosen to walk was bound to please him one way or another. And in return, God made everything easier for her. He turned every obstacle she encountered into a feat of perseverance; such is the fruit the faithful servants of God get.

Yvette's story proves what many may have considered only a myth. Following God's will and obeying Him is the only right way to live, as life in this world is temporary and should only be treated as a test. If we remain firm in our worship and obey God, the reward is eternal life in Paradise. This life is meaningless and doesn't even account for being a shell of what's yet to come. It should be lived only to achieve the goodwill of God and gain our place in Paradise.

Coming to Port-Au-Prince was only the beginning of her adventure, and it was time for Yvette to start her professional career. She would've to work hard to prove her mettle. Now the real challenge will begin as she will be responsible for earning a living, managing her requisites and facing the real world.

Chapter 2
The Capital of Haiti

"Lord, save us! Lord, grant us success!"
– Psalm 118:25

Compared to the small rural community I grew up in, the capital city of Haiti was a teeming, hustling, and bustling metropolis. It seemed as though individuals never had the chance to pause and reflect on the here and now since their lives were perpetually hectic and fast-paced to such an extent that it gave the impression that they were always thinking about the things that happened in the past.

After graduating from the School of Commerce, also known as the Ecole de Commerce Julien Craan, I immediately began submitting applications for positions in various fields within the labor market. Since they pay well and provide significant perks, I would prefer jobs in the public sector.

Soon after I began looking for work, I was fortunate enough to obtain employment as a typist in the Statistics Department of Public Health.

The job was fun and challenging as I needed to type at least 30 words per minute. I was also responsible for performing secretarial work and assisting other seniors with day-to-day activities.

I was a conscientious worker while I was there. I have always made it a point of necessity to obey the rules and kept a close eye out for any revisions or additions to the employee handbook. I believe it was my responsibility to do so. I had enough self-respect to realize that to receive respect from others, I had to respect myself first. Only after I did so, people acknowledged my value and treated me with the care I deserved.

My primary goal in this life has always been to behave in a manner which is commendable and considerate toward others. When I was kind to others, I never expected to get anything in return because I believed those close to me deserved to be treated with respect. And since childhood, my parents instilled in me that I shouldn't expect anything in return for my actions.

My employment did wonders for me. For the first time, I wasn't dependent on anybody or anything. I had the financial means and other resources essential for leading a life of plenty, and I made the most of each one of its precious moments. It appeared as though God was rewarding me at every turn in my life for the effort I put forth, and I was very grateful. Having the experience of holding a job and earning a living is a blessing in disguise, and I can't adequately express my gratitude to God for granting me so much. I had the impression that the money I was bringing in did not solely belong to me; instead, it was a blessing from God that enabled me to contribute to the well-being of my loved ones.

Although some may believe as I gained my independence, I started spending more money, it doesn't reflect the truth. Since I was bringing in a significant amount of cash, I reached to the conclusion it would be advantageous to spend it with frugality and not waste even a single penny. Initially, it was challenging but was essential. If I hadn't done that, there's no way I would've been able to move to the States and start life from scratch there.

Good salary with other incentives was one of the most appealing aspects of my job, and considering I was paid in American dollars made it even more attractive. It is true a different currency and fluctuating exchange rates assisted me in the accumulation of a sizeable fortune. I wasn't spending a lot of money, but I was unable to resist from doing something that's still one of my greatest passions: *Traveling*. All this hard work and efforts would've gone to waste if I refuse to take pleasure in my life.

I've been to many places all across the world and have gathered various experiences throughout my life. My enthusiasm for discovering new localities and experiencing the wonders the world has to offer has been a source of encouragement and support in my life. Regardless of being a woman, it was in me to be able to accomplish anything, and all glory to God for that. I had the confidence of doing whatever good I desired. The freedom I felt while traveling was unlike, and it led me to opening doors that still helps me lead a life that is rich, straightforward and rewarding. If I hadn't spent so much of my life exploring new places, I would've never realized how important it's to find a serene place to settle down and think. Because He did not abandon me when I was in a tough spot and made me believe good things come to those who are good, I have a lot of gratitude and thanksgiving for God. I am so thankful that He is the God who created this universe and took our responsibility.

Making use of this opportunity, I want to discuss some fundamental principles that hold value to me. Thank you for giving me the chance to do so. It all started with the solid moral foundation my parents instilled since I was a child. They raised me well and inculcated proper etiquette and ethics by loving me. However, simultaneously they also knew when to be strict and pull my strings. As a result, my upbringing was healthy with instillation of values and morale one should've. They advised me to always conduct myself in an ethical manner as this was one of the most important principle. Curiosity might arise in a few people when a question like this surfaces up, "Who is a good person?" While there'll be others who might think they are upright and good people. It's not as simple as that; to know if you're a good person, one needs extensive knowledge of the inner workings of the heart and mind, in addition, a life that has been lived with the principles established by God.

At all times, a reasonable person should treat their fellow humans with the same level of respect, care, and compassion they expect for themselves. The act of showing respect to another person conveys to that you value them and consider them to be worthy human beings, deserving of respect. They will take this as a message that you believe in treating them with respect. A compassionate person is who is able to empathize with the suffering endured by other people. It inspires people to reach out and lend a helping hand with the hope of easing the suffering someone is going through. A good person is sympathetic toward the people in their immediate environment and actively seek out ways to assist those struggling to make ends meet. It is possible to bring happiness to those lives which are enduring hard times by demonstrating compassion toward others in difficult spots. In addition to those qualities, it cultivates feelings of understanding, consideration, and support in its beneficiaries.

Furthermore, to this, decent individuals are able to look past the wrongdoings of others, forgive and learn to let go. They don't hold grudges against those who have wronged them and are able to let go of the anger that might compel them to do something which would cause harm to others. They maintain a constructive outlook on life and keep their mental energy directed toward improving the quality of the connections they have around them. They make efforts to refrain from dwelling on the wrongs they have committed in the past or on the affronts that've been committed by others. They have shifted their focus to finding ways to forgive one another so they can also move on with their lives.

Honesty and dependability are two characteristics essential to the definition of a good person. This indicates they steer clear of any scenario where the other person could be harmed, such as spreading rumors, telling lies, or disclosing secrets. Additionally, they need to steer clear of circumstances where they might end up in danger. If they don't engage in any covert behavior, it is impossible to have any reservations about their character or personality. Because of this, there is no longer any room for such uncertainties. They exhibit behaviors which are forthright and truthful, and they shine a light on the genuine personalities and characters they own. People who're deserving of praise are courteous and respectful to everybody around. They help others without anticipating anything in return and put in a lot of effort to make other's lives as satisfying as possible. They don't classify anyone differently depending on parameters such as social background, their appearance, or gender identity. In addition, they don't discriminate against anyone. Good people don't engage in actions such as racism, bigotry, the suppression of others rights, theft, lying, or unethical business practices. Such characteristics don't vouch for people with good character.

People who've good character are courageous in their actions and have an optimistic view of the world as a just and lovely place to live. They have the optimism in them that the world is a wondrous place where everyone receives equal treatment and opportunities. The morally upright is of the opinion individuals are free to choose whether they want to make the world a better or worse place to live in. They live their lives in ways that are beneficial to society as a whole, and they try to make a difference by their contributions.

For instance, as an act of environmental conservation, they make sure that the surrounding area is kept clean for the sake of children and grandchildren who will come after them. One of the most widespread fallacies about people working to protect the natural world is they aren't morally upright and instead are merely enthusiastic about the subject matter. This assumption, on the other hand, is flawed and not supported by facts in any way. People are motivated to care for the environment because of the inherent goodness existing within them. They aren't only concerned about themselves but also about the generations that will follow. They aren't cruel or self-absorbed but rather generous and concerned for the well-being of others.

Those who're morally upstanding share a number of characteristics that set them apart from others. Trustworthiness, honesty, compassion, understanding, forgiveness, respect, courage, and goodwill toward others are examples of these qualities. People who are God-fearing refrain from engaging in behaviors such as stealing, lying, engaging in discriminatory practices, and denying the rights of others. They advocate for policies and procedures that will make the world a better place and are concerned about the well-being of others. They work to ensure that justice and fairness are maintained because they view every person as a worthy and deserving fellow human being. This motivates them to take action toward fostering good in this world.

When I think deeply, I realize I've taken all of these admirable traits into consideration throughout the entirety of my life. In addition, I beseech those who will come after us to appreciate the significance of the aforementioned sentiments and to internalize them as much as we have. It is a blessing from God to be a good person, and everyone ought to make it a goal of theirs to be blessed by God.

My life in the capital was going smoother than ever, and making matters better; it was time for me to be married. My husband was a man like none other. He valued the same sentiments and beliefs as I did, which truly made my decision to marry him so much better. We got married in the year 1978; it was the best day of my life.

The wedding was only attended by close family and friends. We didn't make a big deal out of the occasion at all. Our immediate family, along with a few close friends got together and organized a minimal celebration. We both had a lot of positive thoughts and aspirations regarding the future. We made the decision to devote everything to the life we are building together, and we don't regret that choice.

Although the country descended into anarchy as a direct result of the Anti-Duvalier campaign, I was fortunate enough to be on vacation in Puerto Rico at the time, and I was able to avoid being caught in the crossfire.

Since fortune seemed to be on my side, I reasoned it would be in my best interest to relocate to the United States and carry on living a prosperous life there. Majority of my family and friends had already relocated before I arrived. Some of them had even begun the moving process. In the grand scheme of things, it was time for me to start a new chapter in the journey I call life.

Chapter 3
Life in The United States of America

"*For I was hungry, and you gave Me something to eat; I was thirsty, and you gave Me something to drink; I was a stranger, and you invited Me in.*" – *Matthew 25:35*

My life was at a crossroads, and I had two options: I could continue living in the capital of Haiti as I had been doing up until that point, or I could start a new chapter in my story and move to the United States. I went with the second option. I needed to take control of the situation myself.

Coming to the United States was a choice I made for many different reasons.

Every year, hundreds of thousands of individuals from all over the world attempt to enter the United States of America. Some people are efficacious, while others are not. Despite this, those who don't succeed will likely give it another shot the following year.

The high standard of living in the United States is one of the primary allures for tourists from other countries. Many people dream of settling in the United States, most notably in one of its major cities, such as New

York or Los Angeles. In addition to other things, the United States is home to a thriving entertainment, technological, and nightlife scene. People in tropical regions frequently express their interest in traveling to the United States to experience the snow. In addition, the Federal Government of the United States assists the needy by distributing food stamps and providing access to medical care for those who qualify.

The United States of America has historically been the nation of choice for people who wish to chase their goals. After all, it's known as the land of opportunities. Despite the many recessions that have hit the economy, this country continues to have the most dynamic economy in the world. There is an all-time high number of available jobs for people to choose from. You'll need to move to the United States of America to realize the American dream you've always had.

The situation is currently chaotic in many countries of the third world, including those in Africa, the Caribbean, and the Middle East. Given these nations' dangers and appalling living conditions, it is easy to see why people would need to flee those places. The United States of America, also known as the "land of the free," has historically been the nation of choice for people looking to start a new life for themselves.

People trying to escape from countries currently experiencing war continue to immigrate to the United States year after year in the hopes of a better life. They assimilate rapidly into society and quickly establish themselves as valuable contributors to the community in which they live.

The educational establishments in the United States are widely regarded as some of the most prestigious anywhere in the world. Numerous students submit their applications for student visas to the United States each year in the hope of attending and graduating from one of the country's most prestigious educational institutions. They have two options: they go back to their native country with their degrees in hand, or they decide to stay in the United States and start their professional and family life.

Moving to the United States is not going to be simple for anyone, regardless of their desire; doing so calls for an incredible amount of self-motivation and confidence in one's capabilities. As a new resident of the United States, I, too, needed to prepare myself mentally for the difficulties that lay ahead. Emigrants who opt to come to the USA must face and manage multiple challenges.

The American mentality does not lend itself well to acquiring multiple languages. It can be challenging for visitors who cannot communicate in English to adapt to the way of life in this country. Obtaining a job and making new friends can be just as challenging as performing even the most basic tasks, such as grocery shopping or filling out forms. Immigrants frequently enroll in English as a Second Language (ESL) programs, regardless of doing it with also maintaining a career and caring for children can be challenging. It is significantly more challenging for individuals who cannot read or write in their mother tongue.

The most significant obstacle that immigrants must overcome is learning how to raise children in a new culture. It is not unusual for parents to observe their children rapidly adopting aspects of American culture that are strikingly dissimilar to the culture they were raised in. In addition, studies have shown that children can learn English much faster than adults. Because of this, the relationship between the parent and child is strained, and children, especially adolescents, take advantage of this.

When it comes to school, many parents are disheartened to see their children fall behind their peers' academic performance. In addition, many of these parents report that their children are bullied and discriminated against because of their ethnicity. It is common practice to group children according to their chronological age rather than their actual abilities. This makes it extremely difficult for children who don't speak English to keep up with their peers. To make matters even more difficult, some parents don't have the education or language skills necessary to assist their children, and they may also be unable to communicate with their children's teachers and professors to find a solution to the problem.

When immigrants first arrive in a new country, most are eager to accept any available job. Nevertheless, securing gainful employment and making one's way up the ranks of a large corporation is not easy. They will have a more tough time finding work if they cannot communicate in English effectively. This is especially the case for jobs that involve physical labor. Immigrants who are well-educated and had successful careers in their home countries find it frustrating that they cannot get jobs in the same fields in the United States. Employers give preference to candidates who have gained experience in the United States, and certifications obtained in other countries are rarely acknowledged in this country. As a result, it is not uncommon to find immigrants working in construction with a background in other professions, such as teaching or engineering.

Additionally, immigrants are at a greater risk of being exploited and discriminated against in the workplace. Because of the importance of their jobs to these workers, many employers will pressure them to perform duties that are not only less desirable but also potentially hazardous. Particularly vulnerable to exploitation are immigrants who lack legal documentation and workers who cannot communicate in English.

Finding housing that is both safe and reasonable can be difficult at times. Working jobs that pay a low wage makes it even more challenging to achieve this goal. Many individuals from large immigrant families choose to live in small living arrangements to reduce the stress and distractions of living in close quarters with many extended family members. Immigrants are also vulnerable to being exploited by landlords, particularly those who have recently arrived in the country.

It is especially challenging for undocumented immigrants to obtain assistance because many are afraid of seeking it out for fear of being deported should they do so. Therefore, even when they need assistance, people will put off going to the doctor or seeking assistance from professionals such as lawyers. Even those with the right to be in this country are not assured of their protection here. They are unable to communicate in English, have trouble requesting time off from work, and have few options available to them when it comes to transportation.

Finding assistance for problems related to mental health is especially challenging. Immigrants are frequently the targets of violent crimes, but they may be unsure how or where to seek assistance. To make matters even more difficult, discussing issues related to mental health is considered impolite in many cultures.

Even for those who successfully acquire the required services, the experience leaves a general feeling of dissatisfaction. Because of language barriers, law enforcement officers and medical professionals may incorrectly interpret a victim's statement or incorrectly diagnose a patient.

Language barriers are one of the many aspects of an immigrant's life, that difficulties can negatively impact transportation. Obtaining a driver's license is extremely challenging for various reasons, and this is true regardless of whether or not the application is documented. Those who aren't fluent in English must have a translator present, and finding such people can be quite challenging. For drivers to pass the written test, literacy of a certain level is required.

Even in households with the good fortune to share a vehicle, it can be difficult to transport all family members to and from their respective employment and schools. When men are in charge of keeping the car keys, women are frequently compelled to rely on their male friends or coworkers' generosity to reach their destination. You can probably fathom how challenging it is to accommodate additional responsibilities such as English as Second Language classes and medical appointments when so many people depend on a single vehicle. While many immigrants rely on public transportation as their primary mode of transportation, the experience of using this mode of transportation can be extremely nerve-wracking for others.

Despite their challenges, people who immigrate to the United States are resilient and grateful for the opportunity to live here. They are all motivated by the same goals: they want nothing more than for their children to achieve academic success and for them to be able to provide for their families in the future. They are willing to do whatever it takes to ensure their families' financial stability in this unfamiliar yet intriguing and exciting country.

I want to add myself personally to the list of individuals who are thankful and will continue to be thankful for the chance to gain this experience and participate in this opportunity.

My family members, who were already residing in the United States, were there to greet me when I arrived at the airport. Before that, I was asked to wait an hour for the immigration officials to give me an all-clear signal. My trip and experience, thanks to the All-Powerful God, were both extremely comfortable, and more importantly, they were free of unfortunate events and accidents. In addition to myself, two other family members came to the USA with me.

As I've mentioned, life in this country can be quite challenging for immigrants. Finding a residence to live in that was both affordable and suitable was a difficult task in itself. I was looking for a location where I could start a family. My mother and father were a huge help to me in this regard. They assisted me financially and in making the transition to life in the United States, which was very helpful. I had put aside a significant amount of money, which proved essential in acquiring a visa and, subsequently, a location in the United States of America.

My first step was to investigate several locations and States here. My primary objective was to locate a home that would be suitable for my family. I made an effort to gather as much information as possible on various topics, including the cost of living, various modes of transportation, and the cost of various utilities. After much consideration, I decided to settle in Boston, which is located in Massachusetts.

I gained much information concerning the city of Boston. The cost of living was extremely high in this location. I needed to have my own car to travel from one location to another. I was aware that if I didn't find work soon, I wouldn't be able to continue residing in this location for very long.

English was a must to live a life in America. I came to the deduction that the greatest way for me to improve my English was to enroll in ESL classes. After I had brought my English-speaking abilities up to par, it was time for me to start looking for work. I submitted my resume to the Maristhill Nursing Home. I succeeded in getting the job, and it is one of my proudest accomplishments. I can still intensely recall the sensation of receiving my first paycheck from there; I was simultaneously filled with joy and a sense of accomplishment. Later on, after I had been employed there for some time, I applied to work as a Med Tech at the State of Massachusetts Walter Fernald State School. I was delighted to be handed this chance to work here. It was my occupation up until the day I retired.

I attended training classes at the Financial Academy to become proficient in managing my finances in the United States. My first home was on Union Street in Everett, Massachusetts, and thanks to the education I received from taking those classes, I could purchase it. Later on, I ended up losing the house, but in a way, I was glad about it because it meant that I no longer needed to pay the mortgage. After I retired, I began receiving benefits from my social security and retirement fund, which supported me greatly. The two checks that I received made it possible for me to carry on living a good life with the help of God by my side. It was the second time that I had the experience of feeling true happiness and success in the United States. The first occasion was when I received my first paycheck and was hired for my first job in this location. I want to relay my profound gratitude to God for making that possible.

During the time I spent living in the States, I made several trips to Haiti. I started to miss my motherland and my heritage, so it became important for me to keep in touch with them. The traditions, customs, language, and even the normal day-to-day living I was accustomed to in Haiti are very different from what I experienced in this country. The culture here is very different from what I observed in Haiti. I had several feelings of reminiscence and missed my old life in Port-au-Prince, but I didn't let those feelings ever define who I was. I took accountability for my actions and decided to carry on living my life in the United States.

Somerville was where my children's educational careers began, and they went on to complete their secondary education there. After purchasing my home on Union Street, both of my children started attending Everette High School to finish their education. My son, Richard, attended Bunker Hill Community College and then transferred to ITT University, where he earned a computer science and engineering diploma. Richard is now an engineer. A major company in Massachusetts currently employs him. Keshia, my daughter, decided to attend college for business.

I take great pride that my children and their children have established themselves as contributing members of society in the United States. They have developed into optimistic, well-mannered, and successful individuals; a huge credit goes to their upbringing. My grandchildren have a stable foundation because of their parents' efforts, which overlays the way for them to have an opportunity for a good education and a successful life.

My entire life in the United States has been guided by the principle that I should never engage in immoral behavior. In my opinion, immoral behavior can take on a variety of forms. For me, an act is immoral if done to go against the will of God. I made it a priority to serve in some capacity at the Church and to attend services there regularly. I have never picked up a cigarette because I believe it goes against the very spirit of what it defines as a human being. Alcohol has no place in my life because it clouds people's judgment of God and leads them further away from him.

Going to the park and playing with my grandchildren is one of my favorite things. I believe that to have a healthy mind, we must have a healthy body. Even though I get plenty of water and try to eat healthy diets, the routine that I value the most is ensuring I get enough sleep each night. Regular prayer to God helps me maintain my mental steadiness and keeps me alert. I want to relay my thankfulness to God for the life he has given me.

My life has not always been like this; it has been a journey, and along this journey, the events that took place not only made me stronger but, more importantly, they made my faith in the will and wisdom of God the strongest it could be.

After everything that life throws at us, it is important to remember that God is with the virtuous and will never abandon them.

Chapter 4
Faith

"For the word of God is living and active and sharper than any two-edged sword, and piercing as far as the division of soul and spirit, of both joints and marrow, and able to judge the thoughts and intentions of the heart." – Hebrews 4:12

Many wonders how I was able to endure everything so graciously and happily. Not everything that happened to me or my family was fine and good; as such were times when God put me through his tests and tested my faith. I endured, smiled, and above all, believed it was still a blessing to be chosen among those tested by God's light.

My son had to go through hell due to the evil acts of a woman who deceived him; it was Satan's work; it did not destroy my faith; instead, it made it more robust, for if evil exists, then the light of God encompasses and gains victory over it all, for He is all just and Omnipotent.

I went on many journeys, visited many places, and saw the pyramids. All at once, I was reminded that God gives strength to us to conquer and counter all tribulations, and if we persevere and continue with our heads held high in the mighty light of God, then none can defeat us, for we have faith in our hearts.

My travels took me to Jerusalem, and there I was truly enlightened as I felt my bond and connection to God getting stronger, and in that, I found my eternal peace that whatever happens, I am saved and blessed.

Throughout my life, the Bible has been my crucial companion; it has always guided and nourished me with the information I had lacked forever. Out of all the verses, some have impacted me the most, and I believe they are necessary to live a life full of God's loving grace.

Jesus Christ, God's very word, can be found in every book of the Bible. His perfect nature is diametrically opposed to our own. His keen vision uncovers all the filth that lives in the corrupt hearts of men. His Truthful Word reveals my selfishness, hypocrisy, insincerity, and lack of faith.

God is the God of living who gives us breath and in Whom are the words of eternal life, so His Word has life and power. God's word has real-world effects. It's incredibly miraculous and full of life. The Essence of God is the eternal source of power, and it was through the inspiration of the holy men of God that we have received His supernatural message in the form of the Bible.

"Blessed is the One who does not walk in step with the wicked or stand in the way that sinners take or sit in the company of mockers, but whose delight is in the law of the Lord, and who meditates on his Law Day and night. That person is like a tree planted by streams of water, which yields its fruit in season and whose leaf does not wither — whatever they do prospers. Not so the wicked! They are like chaff that the wind blows away. Therefore, the wicked will not stand in the judgment, nor sinners in the assembly of the righteous. For the Lord watches over the way of the righteous, but the way of the wicked leads to destruction."

— Psalm 1

A beautiful truth is presented right at the beginning of the Psalms: The Lord watches over the virtuous's path, but the wicked's way leads only to destruction. On the other hand, Godliness brings blessings from above, inner contentment, and hope for the future, while ungodliness and compromise lead to a man's ruin and death. It is said that this man is present in the world but unaffected by its superficialities. Such a man would not agree with those who openly reject God and His Messiah. The man of God spoken of in this verse has been redeemed from his sins and is now walking in the truth and the spirit. He stays away from the wicked and their schemes and doesn't associate with sinners. A man like that seeks God's will, studies the Bible, and never takes his eyes off Jesus.

A person like this has good judgment in their daily routines and is careful with their words. A person who lives this way devotes time each day to sitting at Jesus' feet and learning from the Master about God's will for their life, obeying the Lord's commands, and being guided by the Holy Spirit. He delights in the Lord's law and seeks to grow in his knowledge of it. He delights in the Lord, dwells on Him continually, and treasures the wisdom in God's Word. A believer in the Father of Compassion looks down on the things of this world and is willing to die for his carnal wants.

A once godly person can fall into sin in a single verse. They abandon their path of spirit and follow the counsel of men who lead them astray. They eventually give in to the temptations of the world, the flesh, and the devil. Taking one's focus off of Jesus and onto human wisdom can cause a Christian's spiritual enthusiasm to wane to the point where they're more willing to base their convictions on the opinions of evil men than on the truth of God's Word. The longer a Christian spends in the company of ungodly people, the more quickly their conscience will begin to be seared, and the Holy Spirit will be quenched and grieved.

The Bible is the last written record of God's instructions for humankind. It lays out God's intentions and purposes for humanity. Whoever finds delight in the Lord and His Word will have all their wishes granted.

The Lord Jesus Christ should occupy the first place in our hearts and minds, and everything else should flow from that. And we discover that the Christian who reads, marks, learns, inwardly digests, and meditates day and night on the Lord's Word doesn't conform to the world's standards of behavior.

Walking in the counsel of the wicked, keeping company with them, and taking part in their secret deeds of darkness are all indicators that a man is not blessed but rather that he is conjoining himself with the bad people. We live in a fallen world, but our spirits do not; because of what Christ has done for us, we aren't subject to the same arguments, jokes, or conversations as the rest of the world, nor are we obligated to engage in the same shady dealings.

This is not a call to isolate ourselves from the world; instead, we are to be the lights in a dark world, bearing witness to a generation of lost souls about the reality of sin, the importance of righteous living, and the certainty of the Day of Judgment. We must be a living testimony of God's goodness and grace through faith in the Lord Jesus Christ, so the enemy camp does not compromise the integrity of God's glorious gospel.

Spiritual sustenance and renewal are guaranteed for the man who believes in the Lord. His faith is unshakeable because it is grounded in the truth of God's Word, and his fortitude comes from all of God's unlimited resources.

The Lord abides in the man who puts his trust in Christ, and that man produces the lovely fruit of righteousness in the best possible way. Through the indwelling power of the Holy Spirit, his words, deeds, attitudes, and motives are all grounded in God's Word and bring glory to His holy name.

The blessed person's faith remains unshaken even when faced with severe adversity. They can't lose to the enemy's trickery if they're armed with the power of light. They won't be shaken because they have found refuge in the rock of salvation and are protected by His wings.

We would be lost without the Lord Jesus as our constant companion. He has experienced trials that can shake our confidence in God and make us discouraged and worn out. God cares about every thorn in our lives that leaves a deep scar on our souls, as a shepherd cares about his lost sheep.

The righteous man is self-aware of his depravity but confident that God sent His Son to die on the cross for mankind's sins. He believes Jesus was crucified, buried, and rose from the dead on the third day because of what he has read in the Bible.

Praise God; he sent Jesus to show us the way to holiness. Because God knows our path and has always intended to draw us closer to Himself through the trials inflicting our soul and the inevitable "child-training" we will face in life, we can say with Job, "I have heard of You with my ears, but now I see You with a deeper spiritual understanding."

"The Lord is my Shepherd; I lack nothing. He makes me lie down in green pastures,

He leads me beside quiet waters; he refreshes my soul. He guides me along the right paths for his name's sake. Even though I walk through the darkest valley, I will fear no evil, for you are with me;

Your rod and your staff, they comfort me. You prepare a table before me in the presence of my enemies.

You anoint my head with oil; my cup overflows. Surely your goodness and love will follow me all the days of my life, and I will dwell in the house of the Lord forever."

–Psalm 23

The Psalm, often used as a great comfort in times of death or grief, also points to the Lord Jesus Christ as our sustenance and support in every season of our lives, which was done by divine design. Since the Lord is our Shelter and Strength. God alone is our source of fortitude and stability. God alone justifies and rewards his people.

Each of us is like a sheep in the pasture of our good and faithful shepherd, who leads and guides us gently in the way we should go. He is aware of everything we require and knows each of our names. He's also wise to the perils and challenges threatening everyone.

No matter how tumultuous and unsettling our lives may get, He is the One who will guide us to the still-water pools of refreshment. He is the Water of Life, and in Him is found rest for the soul, rest for all who traverse this world in the paths of righteousness on their way to our heavenly home. He is a gushing spring of solace, and He leads us gently by the still waters of His presence. God's city is rejoicing because of His streams, and His people are rejoicing because of His pools of refreshment. He knows just when to pull us aside to rest.

87uIt would be foolish to look for water in this world's stagnant pools and broken cisterns when we have a heavenly Shepherd who provides for all our needs. It would also be careless to let ourselves be swept away by the floods of fancy knocking at our doors or get caught up in the whirlpools of life's disasters. Take this to heart, for the storms are raging, and waves of disaster, disappointment, and trouble are crashing all around us. Reaching out to the Lord and letting Him take your hand and lead you beside the calm, revitalizing, refreshing waters of His love is significant.

In these trying times we are all experiencing, the power of these words has not diminished. Instead, we find that the more we think about these uncomplicated truths, the more weight they gain in our lives, for it is in contemplating these reassuring words that we see the familiar face of Jesus, who has taken on the role of Good Shepherd for us. And He leads us inexorably along the unending grace, peace, righteousness, and love.

When we first put our confidence in Christ alone for our great salvation, He brought our dead spirits back to life through the revivifying power of His death and resurrection. When we're weary from the weight of the world, when we find that we're exhausted, hurt, anxious, or just plain worn out from this troubled life, he is there to restore our fading soul and reinvigorate our sagging spirit.

In the same way, many other promises throughout Scripture have brought comfort to untold millions of believers; these lovely words assure us of restoration, guidance, protection, and peace. He does this for our benefit in the afterlife so we can sing in the praise of his holy name.

The profound impact the Psalm has always had on the lives of those who read it, study it, and take its lessons to heart remains unchanged. For those who follow the Good Shepherd, who laid down his life for the sheep, the valley of the shadow of death becomes a way to life and peace.

The Son of Righteousness illuminates the path of all Who have become sons of light, and the once-dark valley is flooded with light and hope. And as we travel the road God has laid for us, let us put our faith in Him regardless of the difficulties we may encounter: "For Thou art with me. Both the rod and the staff, which are the symbols of the law of the Lord, comfort me.

This Psalm paints a beautiful picture of God as our good and faithful Shepherd, leading us beside peaceful streams. Indeed, he is deserving of our highest adoration and praise. In the face of our adversaries, He is the rock that holds us up, the Provider that calms our fears, and the Blesser that showers us with blessings and provisions. And it is He who makes intercession for us with the father.

Furthermore, God is portrayed as the One who gives rain to the earth, food to the ravens, a protector to the helpless, and justice to the widow in both the Old and New Testaments. For a while, we were still sinners; God, in His grace, provided a Kinsman-Redeemer to save His people from their sins. This God who fed the hungry multitude, comforted the grieving, helped the helpless, strengthened the discouraged, and brought hope to the needy is also the God who saves those who put their faith in Jesus Christ. Through Christ, our Lord and Savior, the good and loving God, provide for all of our needs.

We are surrounded by a generation increasingly corrupt and sinful, but God's peace in Christ Jesus has given us the strength to persevere. We are comforted by His unending love, symbolized by the oil of anointing poured over our heads. We have been given the authority of kings and priests before the living God, and the assurance that His Word is accurate and His promises are "Yes" and "Amen" in Christ because of this precious promise. Like David, we can confidently declare, "My cup of blessing runneth over," because God's grace is infinite, His love is boundless, and His mercy lasts forever.

"The earth is the Lord's, and everything in it, the world, and all who live in it; for he founded it on the seas and established it on the waters. Who may ascend the mountain of the Lord? Who may stand in his holy place? The One who has clean hands and a pure heart, who does not trust in an idol or swear by a false god. They will receive blessing from the Lord and vindication from God, their Savior. Such is the generation of those who seek him, who seek your face, God of Jacob. Lift up your heads, you gates; be lifted up, you ancient doors, that the King of glory may come in. Who is this King of glory? The Lord is strong and mighty, the Lord mighty in battle. Lift up your heads, you gates; lift them up, you ancient doors, that the King of glory may come in. Who is he, this King of glory? The Lord Almighty— he is the King of glory."

– Psalm 24

The glorious arrival of the King of Glory in the holy city of Jerusalem is foretold in Psalm 24. This future King of glory is the unchanging Lord of Hosts, as we are reminded. All humanity ultimately answers to Him because He is the universe's great Creator and unseen Sustainer.

This incredible claim that "the earth is the LORD'S, and the fullness thereof" appears in the first verse and serves as a declaration of the Lord's ownership of the entire planet and all that exists within its borders. God, our Savior, owns the whole world and everyone in it. David boldly states: "The earth and everything in it are the Lord's." Everyone who lives in it belongs to God because he owns the world.

Although brief, Psalm 24 is jam-packed with exultation, information, and praise for the King of glory. In it, the ancient prophets testify to the enthusiastic welcome the Lord God Almighty will receive in the Holy City of Jerusalem upon establishing His heavenly kingdom on earth.

Those who seek God's presence, put their faith in His Word, and have had their hearts cleansed by the word's cleansing water will be blessed. This blessing from the Lord is reserved exclusively for those who God's grace has saved through faith. From the Lord, our Savior, they will receive robes of righteousness.

With prophetic foresight, we can, however, see that this jubilant welcome anticipates the second coming of Christ Jesus, our Lord, to establish His kingdom on Earth. In due time, the King of Glory will enter the city of Jerusalem for His glorious coronation, and all the righteous will be overjoyed at this news. Only those who have faith in Him and have washed their hands and hearts clean can enter the Holy place.

His kingdom, in contrast to the temporary monarchies of this world, will last forever. God's Anointed King and the long-awaited Messiah, the King of Glory, is strong and mighty to save, in contrast to the petty tyrants of the Earth brought low by God's sovereign authority. He is the Son of God, and as such, he will rule the world justly until all his enemies are crushed, and the kingdom is restored to God the Father. Honor His glorious name.

"The Lord is my light and my salvation— whom shall I fear? The Lord is the stronghold of my life—of whom shall I be afraid? When the wicked advance against me to devour me, it is my enemies and my foes who will stumble and fall. Though an army besieges me, my heart will not fear; though war breaks out against me, even then, I will be confident. One thing I ask from the Lord, this only do I seek: that I may dwell in the house of the Lord all the days of my life, to gaze on the beauty of the Lord and to seek him in his temple. For in the day of trouble, he will keep me safe in his dwelling; he will hide me in the shelter of his sacred tent and set me high upon a rock. Then my head will be exalted above the enemies who

surround me; at his sacred tent, I will sacrifice with shouts of joy; I will sing and make music to the Lord. Hear my voice when I call, Lord; be merciful to me and answer me. My heart says of you, "Seek his face!" Your face, Lord, I will seek. Do not hide your face from me, do not turn your servant away in anger; you have been my helper. Do not reject me or forsake me, God my Savior. Though my father and mother forsake me, the Lord will receive me. Teach me your way, Lord; lead me in a straight path because of my oppressors. Do not turn me over to the desire of my foes, for false witnesses rise up against me, spouting malicious accusations. I remain confident of this: I will see the goodness of the Lord in the land of the living. Wait for the Lord; be strong and take heart and wait for the Lord."

– Psalm 27

God is our sword and buckler; nothing in all creation, above or below, or in all the waters below the earth, can erase the promises He has made to us. For us, he is the rock upon which our existence rests. Because he is the firm foundation upon which we can safely rest, nothing can shake our confidence in the Lord's unfailing love for us found in Christ Jesus our Lord.

When we permit ourselves to be led and guided by His eternal light, the divine light of a heavenly birth floods our soul, driving away all darkness, soothing our sorrows and fears, and directing us toward the paths of righteousness and truth. In addition to being our Savior, He is also our salvation, strength, peace, and God.

If we take David's lead, walk in the light and trust His Word, we will not be led astray but will have the light of life. Nothing in heaven or earth, seen or unseen, should cause us to lose faith or fear.

Today, many wait in ambush to snare the believer who has put their faith in God. Many people will distort the truth or set a trap to shame or humiliate their target. Faith is unwavering certainty that God's promises are genuine and will be fulfilled in the person of Jesus Christ. That which can only be seen with the eye of faith is the evidence of the reality of the things we have hoped and trusted in the Lord our God with all our hearts.

Having faith in God's promises, which we cannot yet see with our physical eyes but which we can see with the eye of faith, gives us the strength to hope. This quality of David's made the Lord very happy. And David again showed himself to be a man after God's own heart, who trusted the Word of the Lord and believed God would deliver him from the hands of all his enemies.

The future strikes fear into the hearts of men today, but we are not of this world to despair; our faith is in the same God in whom David put his trust. Let us not lose sight of the Blessed Hope, the glorious appearing of our great God and Savior, the Lord Jesus Christ, but rather let us hold fast to the joy that is before us while we wait for it.

Our faith is bolstered when we wait patiently for the Lord to work despite the difficulties we face. On the other hand, during the most trying times in life, our faith is put to trial as we wait patiently in prayer, praise, and thanksgiving for the Lord to act and fulfill His promises.

"God is our refuge and strength, an ever-present help in trouble. Therefore we will not fear, though the earth give way and the mountains fall into the heart of the sea, though its waters roar and foam and the mountains quake with their surging. There is a river whose streams make glad the city of God, the holy place where the Most High dwells. God is within her; she will not fall; God will help her at break of day. Nations are in uproar, kingdoms fall; he lifts his voice, the earth melts. The Lord Almighty is with us; the God of Jacob is our fortress. Come and see what the Lord has done, the desolations he has brought on the earth. He makes wars cease to the ends of the earth. He breaks the bow and shatters the spear; he burns the shields with fire. He says, "Be still, and know that I am God; I will be exalted among the nations, I will be exalted in the earth. "The Lord Almighty is with us; the God of Jacob is our fortress." – Psalm 46

We can run to God and find safety whenever we feel overwhelmed by life's challenges; we can run to God and find safety. In a world that rejects Christ, denies God is anti-Semitic, and is anti-Christian, he is our rock of refuge, stronghold, and tower of strength. But the Lord has given us His unwavering promise that He will be with us and never leave or abandon us, and the God of Jacob is our rock of refuge, our safe stronghold, and our ever-present help in times of trouble.

How many Christians throughout history have found peace and solace in the Lord's presence by resting their minds on these words from the Psalmist? What relief these reassuring words have brought to many sheep who have heard the voice of their Good Shepherd, that Great Shepherd of the sheep who welcomes all who come in His name.

We are to find calm in the truth of God's Word and the holiness of His presence. Through faith and praise, we acknowledge that the Lord is God, the Giver of life and the Redeemer of souls, the One who rescues us from the depths of despair and bestows upon us the crown of His lovingkindness and compassion.

"Surely our griefs He Himself bore, and our sorrows He carried; Yet we ourselves esteemed Him stricken, Smitten of God, and afflicted. But he was wounded for our transgressions, he was bruised for our iniquities: the chastisement of our peace was upon him, and with his stripes, we are healed." – Isaiah 53:4-5

Christ's substitutionary death, burial, and resurrection, as described in Scripture, is the single most spectacular event in all of history and all of eternity because it is through it that God made salvation available to anyone who believes in the name of the only begotten Son of God.

He was blameless and innocent and had basked in the glory of heaven from eternity past, and yet He was willing to be uncovered of His magnificence to save us, who were guilty, lost, dead in our sins, and at enmity with God. He was set to give up His position as the supreme deity in the afterlife. He chose to be born into a human race that has consistently opposed God. So we who put our faith in Him might receive forgiveness of sin and be redeemed from eternal separation from our Creator, He was scourged, humiliated, and put to death.

All of us who have put our faith in Christ as Savior can feel the pain of these words as we contemplate that the holy Son of God voluntarily suffered the bruising, piercing, and crushing wounds that we deserved and then died the death that we deserved. Because our guilt was borne by the spotless Son of Man, our spiritual kin and Redemptor.

Jesus Christ willingly submitted to torture and death so that those who put their faith in Him might have eternal life and peace with God. Let His tranquility watch over our hearts, for it is by His stripes that we are healed, physically, spiritually and eternally.

"I well remember them, and my soul is downcast within me. Yet this I call to mind, and therefore, I have hope: Because of the Lord's great love, we are not consumed, for his compassions never fail. They are new every morning; great is your faithfulness. I say to myself, "The Lord is my portion; therefore, I will wait for him." The Lord is good to those whose hope is in him, to the One who seeks him; it is good to wait quietly for the salvation of the Lord." – Lamentations 3:20-26

When we remember God's unfailing love, we are given reason to hope again. This is more accurate now than ever before. The finished work of Christ on the cross gives us confidence amid life's difficulties. If we believe that God is faithful, we can rest easy knowing that even if our loved ones are taken from us by death, they will have a way into His Kingdom. It is impossible to exhaust God's compassion and forgiveness.

After detailing his struggles and temptations, Christ demonstrates how he ultimately triumphed over them. If things aren't even worse than they are, it's only by God's grace. It's essential to keep an eye on our supporters and detractors. God's mercy never runs out, as evidenced by his continually showering us with new examples each morning. A portion of earthly things will eventually decay, but a portion of God will last forever.

Hoping and patiently waiting for the Lord's salvation is our obligation, and it will bring us comfort and satisfaction. Many young people who might have grown up proud and unruly have benefited from bearing this yoke because it has taught them humility and seriousness and weaned them from the world. If you can learn to be patient through hardship, you'll gain wisdom from experience and find hope in the face of adversity.

If we hold firm to the word of God, then there is nothing that can falter us from the path of those who will walk with Jesus Christ in the heavens above, so my message remains always have faith in God, for he has a plan and his plan is the best thing possible for us, always and forever.

Chapter 5
Family Comes First

"*God sets the lonely in families [the desolate in a homeland], He leads out the prisoners with singing, but the rebellious live in a sun-scorched land." – Psalm 68:6*

Family Life and The Bonds Between Us

When it seems like meaning is being lost along with everything else, it's more crucial than ever to focus on the importance of family. Despite the changes brought about by progress and technology, the value of family and what it represents haven't yet changed. People who share common ancestry or blood ties are considered family. The bonds between these individuals go beyond blood ties; they are also based on shared values of kindness, love, and mutual support. The influences of one's parents and siblings profoundly affect a person's development. Different kinds of families exist in modern society. Family can be further broken down into nuclear families, single-parent families, stepfamilies, grand families, cousins' families, etc.

The term "family" can mean many disparate things, depending on the context. When born into this world, we immediately become part of a family. We call those who nurture and develop us family, and they become indispensable to our survival. A strong family behind you can make all the difference, whether you succeed or fail. It makes no difference what kind of family one comes from. As long as there is love and acceptance, everything is fair game. It doesn't matter if your family structure is unclear, same-sex, or joint. Our family's resilience rests on the foundation of the close bonds we share. The connection we share is unique to us. Among the many pillars of strength in a person's life, the family stands tall as the most important.

Many things contribute to a healthy family unit. The most outstanding value of all is love. When you think of your family, feelings of unconditional love flood your mind, it's the first time you feel truly loved. What it teaches you about love will remain with you always. Second, it's clear that loyalty helps keep families together. Having kids makes you a dedicated family member. You're there for them through the good times and the bad, and you celebrate with them when they succeed. Members of a family always have each other's backs. To show their loyalty to one another, they defend one another from an outsider who threatens them. More importantly, the lessons one learns from one's family strengthen the bonds between family members. For instance, in the context of one's family, we acquire the foundational skills for navigating the world. It's a prodigious way to reinforce our bond with our first teachers. Since our beliefs are familiar to each other, this is one of the ways it unites us. Nobody in your family will ever abandon you, no matter what happens. Whatever trials you face in life, you can count on them to be there to help you through them. If you or a loved one are facing a difficulty of any kind, talking to family members about it, no matter how brief, can help lift your spirits, give you hope, and offer the inspiration you need to keep going.

The value of a strong family unit must be emphasized. They significantly impact our lives and help us grow as people. Those who have families often take them for granted. Those without families to support them know how to recognize a person's true value. We gain our resilience from being part of a family. It enlightens us on the significance of interpersonal bonds. A family facilitates the development of genuine connections with people. We take into our own partnerships what we learn to love and cherish from our families. Family life also helps us develop our communication skills. When we invest in our loved ones, show them our appreciation, and talk to them openly, we improve our chances for a brighter future. Keeping in touch with loved ones helps us develop useful social skills in all aspects of life.

Similar to how we learn patience from our families. Sometimes it's hard to have patience with close relatives. But we stay that way because we value each other's presence. As a result, it teaches us to be more patient and resilient in our daily lives. The support and affection of family members can do wonders for our self-esteem. They are the rock upon which we can rely and who help us grow into better versions of ourselves. Family is where we learn essential life lessons: how to love and be loved; how to respect and believe in something; how to have faith and hope; how to care about others; how to practice ethical and moral behavior; and how to honor and uphold our cultural traditions. A person's foundation is strengthened when they grow up in a stable family environment. A person's moral compass is honed through family and community. They pick up on the right and wrongdoings of the household and the importance placed on various factors by the neighborhood and larger society.

Generally speaking, culture begins and ends with families. In many households, passing down family tales is a meaningful way to preserve history and culture. This is a great way to maintain relationships with ancestors who have passed on. A child raised in such a home has a strong sense of belonging to a community. They will take pride in living through the ups and downs of their community. When families are solid, communities flourish. Ultimately, this helps build stronger communities and nations. There are a lot of things that add up to a strong family. Being made from love teaches us how to love without conditions. A strong family is built on a foundation of loyalty, which encourages its members to show loyalty to others.

Most importantly, love and acceptance can help a family grow closer together. There is no more incredible unit of social organization or individual fulfillment than the family. As such, they provide invaluable lessons in interpersonal communication and development. They cherish and respect us because of this love. They give us a sense of worth and pride in ourselves. They also help us develop the self-control and tolerance we need to get along with others.

Benefits of Family Life

A child's emotional and physical needs are met by their family. Support from a loved one is often relied on when times are tough. One of the greatest ways to build a foundation of support for a child is to love them unconditionally. As their secure home, they know they can always return whenever necessary. It's essential to talk to one another freely to form lasting bonds. The key to effective communication is allowing all parties, including children, a voice. They should be able to speak their minds freely and respectfully to one another in open conversations. Compromise and consideration for one another's perspectives are cornerstones of a healthy family dynamic. Everyone in the family has a sense of belonging and unity. Numerous studies on family dinners and time have found that sharing a meal has positive and preventative effects on children. Adolescents' mental health, academic success, and communication skills benefit from regular family dinners.

Additionally, it aids in keeping kids from engaging in potentially damaging activities like drug use, violence, sexual activity, and dropping out of school. It's impossible to overstate the significance of family time, but that doesn't mean it shouldn't be of high quality. Relationships can't be strengthened by simply spending more time together. If that were the case, everyone's relationships would be perfect after a lockdown. How we use that time is more crucial. Good times require more than just having a good time together. The best way to spend quality time with a child is to make an effort to be there for them, especially during hard times.

Families lay the groundwork for all subsequent interactions. A child's primary attachments are to their parents and siblings. Whether healthy or not, these connections serve as a template for how we should approach love in the future. Intentionally or not, people choose friends and romantic interests similar to their biological relatives. The patterns of interaction within a family can serve as powerful role models for conducting oneself in interpersonal settings and one's identity development.

People require a supportive family unit most during difficult times. When times are rough, we all need a helping hand. Financial and emotional help is also required. If they know they can rely on their loved ones to support and encourage them, it gets easier for the time to pass. In times of distress, human beings have an innate desire to be surrounded by people who will accept and understand them as it is. That's something both biological and adoptive families can provide to their children.

Life's most valuable lessons are typically learned within a family setting. Children's first experiences with social interaction, communication, and regulation of their emotions occur in the context of their families. It's also the first place a child experiences positive and negative outcomes due to their actions. Parents should teach their kids lessons that'll stick with them for a lifetime. These teachings shape a person's outlook and assumptions about the world.

The values we hold dear are those we learned from our families. People acquire a moral compass and a set of principles through their families, along with life lessons. They pick up on the norms and values of the household and the larger society. People's identities are built on the bedrock of the principles they've internalized throughout their lives. People's values shape their behavior toward others, sense of self-worth, and outlook on life's meaning.

Helping one another out with the basics is why the concept of families was born. As the primary unit of society, the family is responsible for providing for its members who are powerless to do so on their own. Included in this category are either too young to live independently, too old, unable to work to support themselves financially, or both. When one or more family members can provide for the household, necessities like food, water, shelter, and clean air are always within reach.

People in stable households can rest easy knowing their needs will be met by their own families. The first step in ensuring everyone in the family has what they need and want is for everyone who can work to contribute at least some of their income toward that goal. Second, to guarantee their basic needs are always met, the family works together to pay bills and manage their finances.

Some people have fantastic news but nobody to share it with. However, when living with relatives, one rarely encounters such an issue. Some people don't experience the simple pleasures that those raised in stable households do. Moreover, everybody goes through rough patches in their life. People in a happy family look out for one another. Close friends and family members are frequently the first to notice when a loved one is struggling. Even if a person keeps their issues hidden from the general public, their loved ones will usually be the only ones who truly understand. The person loves regardless of whether or not they agree with the loved one's behavior. They offer support to members of the family in difficult times.

When a family is healthy, the children are too. They have access to nutritious food, are prompted to get up and move, are given opportunities to spend time in nature, and are given timely medical care. Parents can also reap health benefits. Having children in the household has been linked to a longer lifespan, and this effect persists even after the children have left their homes. One possible explanation is that parents are more likely to adopt healthier lifestyles than those who don't have children. It can be terrifying to deal with health issues on your own. Family members provide necessities like food, water, shelter, and medical attention, which can alleviate the situation. When a family takes care of its members' needs, the community doesn't have to. And when family members fulfill their responsibilities, the roles are automatically achieved.

Individuals from stable families tend to be productive members of society. Families with children are more likely to volunteer than individuals who live alone. In addition, they instill an early understanding in their kids, which assists their actions in directly impacting the kind of community they grow up in. When parents give back to their communities by providing funds or supplies, they set a positive example. They teach their kids that giving back to the community through monetary contributions, food donations, or other means strengthens the community's ability to provide for its members. A meaningful way that parents make a difference is by working to provide their children with the best educational opportunities they can. They might make a monetary donation or use their connections to find a job for a young adult still in school. It may be more valuable to receive emotional and practical support than financial aid. At least for the vast majority of human history, criminal activity has always been a part of every human society. Even though families can't wholly stop criminal activity, they can work to reduce its frequency and severity.

What Ruins Family Life?

Family life offers many rewards, but it also has its difficulties. It's reasonable you might need some help getting through each day. A relationship problem, such as dissatisfaction with a partner, can trigger negative emotions and even lead to separation and divorce. Before committing to someone, it's best to express your feelings about marriage and having kids. Because of this, their occurrence is restricted. A lot of families have major bad breakdowns, which is sad. This can strain the family dynamic and make everyone feel awkward. The first step in deciding the cause is identifying the underlying issue. Once you do that, you can start considering your options for fixing the problem. Relationships within the family are particularly vulnerable to the destructive effects of insults and criticism. While it may not seem possible, words said with the intention of hurting can leave deep wounds that last a lifetime. Negative comments are especially harmful in family relationships because they come from people who should be your most excellent source of support and encouragement regardless of the times.

It's common to say something carelessly amid an argument, and most people will understand and forgive you. However, the problem is it can cause rifts within families. These conflicts are difficult to resolve and should be avoided. If you can't contemplate something nice to say, then don't say anything. If you feel like speaking up, it's best to do so in a level-headed way that contributes to the conversation rather than resort to personal attacks.

Negative rumors can have a devastating effect on any situation. Usually, when someone gossips about another person, it's mostly due to the problems one may have with the other person. This may help you feel better in the short term, but it will not resolve the underlying issue. When you make up things about someone, they naturally stop trusting you. In addition, it may prompt the rest of the relatives to split and take sides. The family will be even more polarized as a result of this. If you disagree with someone, it's best to discuss it one-on-one. Engage in a reasonable discussion of the problems, their roots, and potential resolutions. If you succeed, your relationship will grow deeper.

The strength of a family depends on everyone feeling like they belong. Everybody in the family should have a say in significant decisions, regardless of whether everyone agrees, because it will make them feel like an integral part of the family. Isolating a family member can cause them to internalize inferiority and resentment. Your family members are free to accept or decline your invitation to any event, outing, or activity you arrange. Strengthening family bonds requires doing what we can to make everyone feel like they belong. A family without any members isn't a family.

Relationships within a family can be severely damaged by deceit and lies. Being lied to can ruin even the healthiest of relationships. Sometimes, the truth may not emerge for decades or even centuries. However, in the end, the truth will always be revealed. Keep that in mind. Who else can you be truthful with, if not your loved ones? Relationships suffer when family members are lied to or even when small secrets are kept. That's because somebody betrayed your trust. The greater the lie, the more harm it causes. Your actions will have consequences, both for you and those around you. That's why it's important to own up to your faults and do what you can to make amends with the ones close to your heart. Being truthful with loved ones is a gesture of immense respect.

As a kid, you have to follow your parents' rules. Everybody in your family is treated the same way and given the same level of instruction and correction. However, this doesn't imply that you're carbon copies of one another. Just because you share a wall with someone doesn't mean you have to agree on everything. Everyone in the household must respect one another's thoughts, preferences, and likes. Family relationships can take a severe hit if you can't avoid getting into fights with other people over their differences. Loving someone means accepting them in their rawest forms.

Genuine regret serves as a powerful adhesive. Apologizing shows you value the other person and don't wish for any animosity to develop between you. Family members need each other at all times. Keeping a grudge in your heart never leads to a positive outcome. To keep harmony in the house, practice and ask for forgiveness whenever you've wronged a family member. It aids in cleaning the hearts and bringing people closer.

Role of Parents in A Family

Parental involvement in their children's education is a crucial social good. Not all education is imparted to the teacher. Learning is a top priority in a happy and healthy family, second only to providing for physical needs. The political opinions of family members are frequently discussed during mealtime conversations. They might argue over who has the best credentials for the upcoming election or what issues need to be addressed so they can cast a knowledgeable vote. This, in turn, encourages everyone to learn more about the candidates and issues.

The parent's test begins at the time of their child's birth. As the child grows, the parents may assist them in learning to walk and introduce them to new words as their language skills advance. They use everyday experiences as teaching opportunities, such as potty training and manners instruction. Most importantly, they instill in their children a thirst for knowledge that will serve them well throughout their lives. Most parents have varying resources for supporting their children's schooling outside the classroom. They have the potential to inspire both scholarly pursuits and moral conduct.

As a parent, it can feel like a huge burden to mediate every argument your kids have with one another. For example, parents can deal with conflict by showing their kids how to work things themselves. Parents instill morality in their offspring and urge them to uphold the law unless they can see how breaking that law will be for the greater good. Cleaning the house is typically a family affair. The more they toil together, the more they learn what it's like to contribute to a common goal.

A child's academic success can be attributed more to their parents' efforts than their attendance at a particular school. If parents assist their children with their schoolwork, the children perform better academically, and the parents can stress the importance of school; more children attend school functions. Briefly put, parents are a child's first and most influential educators. Every aspect of a child's character formation, from morals and manners to discipline and self-control, begins at home. Their positive upbringing sets them up for future endeavors and success.

The educational opportunities of their parents' choice are more important than the quality of their children's schools. When parents are tangled in their children's schooling, they tend to see an improved academic performance. Improving educational opportunities alone will not increase social mobility is one crucial fact. There should also be exertions made to increase parental participation. Family social capital, which refers to how involved parents are in their children's lives, is crucial to a child's success in school; however, school social capital is also equally necessary.

If parents regularly checked their children's homework, talked about school with them, and participated in school activities, such as parent-teacher conferences, they were seen as passing on higher levels of social capital. These are a few examples of how parents impart wisdom and experience to their offspring. Meanwhile, schools with high social capital ensure a positive learning environment that engages students and keeps them returning for more. Students acquire social graces not only at home but also in the classroom.

Many schools try to keep in touch with parents and provide extra-curricular opportunities for their students. When teachers notice a problem, they also talk to the parents. Parents must now play a role in assisting their children's development when the teachers inform them. So, while excellent educational opportunities boost achievement, the influence of the family unit is even more significant. Examination performance for students with low school capital but high family capital is improved. School and family involvement are crucial; family involvement is more decisive regarding academic success. The parental role in a child's education is also crucial. Therefore, parents need to be more vigilant in checking their children's homework, coming to parent-teacher conferences, and emphasizing the significance of education.

Having a role model in the form of a parent is crucial for fostering moral development in children. The things they learn at home are automatically imitated by the child and are never forgotten. Therefore, parenting is not just vital. On behalf of the parents, decent parenting, in turn, ensure a healthier society. If we take the time to instill good morals and ethics in today's youth, maybe they'll grow up to make the world a better place where we can all live in peace and harmony.

My parents have been a continuous basis of support and encouragement for me throughout my entire life. They trained me with the skills I required to become a contributing member of society. They provided me with a solid basis to build my life and imparted invaluable knowledge regarding the workplace and marriage. They were the ones who imparted to me the difference between rights and wrongs and gave me knowledge of having good values. They indoctrinated what it means to be a responsible parent, and I hope to carry on the tradition they established. They educated me on God and showed me how to find meaning and direction in the life of Jesus Christ through the lessons they taught me.

What Does God Say About Family Life?

"Be fruitful and increase in number; fill the Earth and subdue it. Rule over the fish in the sea and the birds in the sky and over every living creature that moves on the ground." – Genesis 1:28

When we take stock of the state of the world today, we see a sad picture. Love of money and materialism are just two examples of the egocentric desires that have plagued our society and humanity. There is an epidemic of broken families, sexuality is distorted in the media, and marital dissolution is the norm. We have contaminated our planet to the extent that a hole is forming in the ozone layer, and as a result, children and their families are dying of hunger. This is the nature of the world we currently find ourselves in. We failed to see God's will for our lives, and as a result, this happened. Genesis 1:28 is the first mention of this scheme. After making the world and determining it was good, God made humans the final part of creation. The God who made them in His image also blessed them. The first words that God speaks to man are found in Genesis 1:28, or the "three great blessings," as I will refer to them. God also repeats these statements 12 times in the book of Genesis.

God made our destinies clear by giving us rules to live by. Since doing what He says will make Him happy, we can take comfort in His words. Fruitfulness, multiplication, and rule over the world are all mandated by his word. However, we've failed to properly implement the three great blessings on many occasions because we've ignored this. Let's analyze the significance of each blessing.

Be fruitful, which means "abundantly productive," were God's first words He ever spoke to Adam. God's first command to humanity was "Be fruitful," a call to develop morally, spiritually, and emotionally so they might "abundantly produce" as He had. With the command, "Be perfect, therefore, as your heavenly Father is perfect," God urged His children to emulate God, the Father. For this reason, having children can be compared to the "dating" phase of life. Today is the day to start or strengthen your relationship with God so you can become a person of honor.

This "multiply" business was God's second request of Adam and Eve. God's proposal all along was for Adam and Eve to join together in holy matrimony, with an emphasis on Him, and to start a lovely family that would serve as a classroom for learning how to love one another. But "multiply" can mean more than just having kids. To instill a love for God in one's offspring is what this phrase refers to. Because we are fallen and cannot guarantee that our offspring will be sinless, it stands to reason that we should also focus on increasing our spiritual progeny. This refers to the process of evangelism, which Jesus taught us about in the New Testament and whose goal is the expansion of the church on Earth.

When a man and woman marry without God as their foundation, they can't create the ideal family God intended. God's original plan for reproduction was for each parent to experience the joy of the birth of someone who'd reflect and magnify their nature and God's. This kind of family would be a bastion of God's rule in the material world and a source of unending affection for one another. God had high expectations for this to happen.

After God has asked us to tend to ourselves and our loved ones, He then requests that we tend to the world around us. In the Garden of Eden, God commanded Adam and Eve to rule over the entire universe. As His gift to humanity, He expects us to treat the natural world with reverence.

Therefore, although "dominion" may seem like a heavy word, God only wants us to take care of our environment, which in turn brings us joy: the Earth, the fish of the ocean, the bird of the air, and every living thing that moves on the Earth. Given His care and love in making them, it's our responsibility and promise to God that we will protect them.

I pray that you have gained a deeper understanding of God's words in Genesis 1:28. The first words God spoke to humanity are profoundly precious. As we learn more about and work toward achieving the three great blessings of "be fruitful, multiply, and have dominion," their significance grows for us personally as well. Of course, God has given us directions and a clear way of life through the many prophets who came before us in the Old Testament and through His Son, Jesus Christ, in the New Testament. However, this is because fallen nature of humankind. Since we are sinners who disobeyed God's first words, He sent His Son to preach a message of love for one's enemies.

To put it another way, we become self-centered and seek out things like power, wealth, and fame because we've neglected to fulfill the first blessing by developing a reliable relationship with God and making Him the focus of our life. This kind of union is impossible to sustain because it excludes God. They won't be ready to put each other first and, instead, will let their desires get in the way. This contributes to problems like sexual immorality, divorce, and broken families. And how could we care for the natural world if we haven't fulfilled the first two blessings of being fruitful and multiplying through a beautiful God-centered family? Caring for Creation would be the furthest thing from our minds if we don't work on ourselves or our relationships with those around us. The lack of ownership over the world's resources has led to an imbalanced focus on the individual gain at the expense of the common good. The three gifts are intertwined.

Instead, we're to be fruitful in our reproduction and ability to exercise dominion over the Earth, as God intended. God desired us to devote our single years to developing our faith, becoming more united with Him and maturing spiritually as we readied our hearts and lives for the mate, He had in store for us. Only when two people have a strong faith in God and have put in the time and energy to improve themselves and their character can they truly become one. When God is at the center of a couple's lives, they are better equipped to resist temptation as a team because they are more likely to put their partner's needs before their own, increasing their chances of having healthy, happy children. One thing that happens when God is at the center of a family is they take better care of the resources God has given them. With each other's help, they can tend to and protect the natural world.

Consequently, no matter where you're in life, you can take baby steps toward fulfilling God's commands that you "Be fruitful" by deepening your union with Him, "Multiply" by building a loving family, and "Dominion" over all Creation by caring for it. Too often, people have ignored God's words in Genesis 1:28, which is why the world is in the state it is in today. However, it is also up to us to follow God's word and change the world for good.

My Constant Prayer

God, please give me strength when I am weak, love when I feel lonely, courage when I am afraid, wisdom when I act foolish, enlighten me when I'm imprudent, comfort me when I am stressed, provide me with hope when I feel rejected, and give me peace when I am in turmoil. Amen.

My Aspirations

Currently, all I want to do is convey my aspirations for the long-term future of my family, as well as my hopes for the continuation of our lineage after many generations have passed. I want them to put God, the creator of everything, at the forefront of everything they do. I want them always to be genuine and never put on an act in real life. I want them to be happy, make the most of their lives, and, most importantly, dream and have aspiration of achieving greatness. I also want them to make the good and most out of their lives. I want them to keep fighting no matter how difficult things get. I don't want them to be hopeless ever because I know those who are patient will ultimately be rewarded. I hope they will appreciate the value of their education and put forth the effort necessary to obtain it, just as their parents have done. In conclusion, I wish for them to become helpful and successful members of society who're able to amass valuable assets and earn a legitimate living. They will leave a legacy that will be carried on by the generations that will come after them, and it is my sincere hope this chain of goodness will continue on into infinity.

Chapter 6
Ethics

Regarding rights, duties, societal benefits, fairness, or particular virtues, ethics is based on canons of right and erroneous suggesting what humans must do. Emotions are often mistaken for ethical judgments. However, morality is not something based on how one feels. It's possible that someone who listens to their emotions would avoid doing the right thing. Ethical considerations often take a back seat to how we feel. Also, morality and faith are two separate concepts. Of course, the majority of faiths promote morality. However, if morality were limited to religious institutions, it would only be relevant to those who identify as religious. However, the principles of ethics apply just as much to the actions of an atheist as they do to a religious fundamentalist. Religion has the potential to both set rigorous moral standards and provides powerful incentives for upholding those standards. Following the law is not the same thing as being ethical. Ethical norms to which the vast majority of people adhere are frequently codified in law. Although legislation, like sentiment, can stray from what is morally right. The laws that allowed slavery in the United States before the Civil War and the apartheid laws still exist in South Africa today are egregious examples of laws against ethical norms. Finally, doing what's considered acceptable is not the same as acting ethically. In any community, most people will adhere to standards generally agreed to be moral. Nevertheless, societal norms may depart from what is ethical. Corruption in ethics can spread throughout an entire culture.

Ethical norms dictate what individuals should do based on considerations of their own or others rights, duties, the common good, justice, or a set of laudable character traits. When we converse about "ethics," we're referring to the rules that tell us we have to be vigilant regarding certain things, such as not committing homicide, not stealing, not assaulting other people, not lying, and not spreading false information. The standards of honesty, compassion and loyalty are all part of ethics. The right to natural life, the right to have freedom from harm, and the right to privacy are all rights addressed by ethical standards. Ethical standards are sufficient because they are backed by coherence and solid evidence. The term "ethics" is used to describe the process of examining and improving one's moral principles. Ethical standards are not always upheld by popular opinion, the law, or social convention. For this reason, it is important to regularly assess one's standards to ensure they're reasonable and grounded in reality. Therefore, the study of ethics also includes the ongoing effort to examine one's moral beliefs and behavior and to ensure that one and the institutions one helps shape adhere to reasonable and sound norms.

Crucial Ethical Values to Have as A Human Being

Being Technologically Competent

The word "technology" frequently appears in contemporary conversation. It is more like a standard scientific term. The two are not the same, though. While the results of fundamental academic studies make up science, technology refers to the practical application of science. Understanding how people acquire new technologies requires accounting for this distinction. Having access to technology can give an individual a strategic advantage that underpins the importance of technology in today's world. In this sense, technology is a strategic asset. Understanding and using technology is also seen as a fundamental skill.

Using technology in the schoolroom may seem like a paradox to you. Even the youngest students usually have a solid foundation when using and navigating modern technology. Students can feel like they are starting to grasp the material by using it in class. Students in today's classrooms are expected to take the instructor at their word and memorize material without actively engaging with the material. Students are more likely to learn and retain information from an interactive lesson. Students gain self-assurance by actively learning through games, online assignments, discussions, and research. Lessening student stress and confusion by making school more enjoyable is a worthy goal. By reducing the emphasis on academics, achievement can be made through classroom games, unstructured group projects, and student-guided research.

Instead of cramming information down students' throats, education should be a more natural process. Students are more likely to work together when given access to online communication and shared technological platforms. The obscurity of email makes it easier for students to seek assistance than in person. For collaboration to affect student performance, students must be connected for course-related work. It is common knowledge that students can accomplish more when they use the internet and work together. Students will develop pride in their intelligence and creativity as they can take on more challenging coursework. They can find answers to your questions if you provide them with a wide range of background material, including access to online resources. Students who learn to solve problems rather than depending on their teachers for assistance report higher satisfaction with their educational experience. Students who might be too shy to speak up in class would be more likely to participate in online discussions or complete online assignments. More reserved students will be more active in class if they get to double-check their answers or respond privately to questions. After gaining experience communicating online, most students will feel more comfortable speaking up in class. Students can take their time and think more carefully about their answers on an online test or assignment because they can go back and look at them. Some kids who don't believe in themselves will gain confidence after hearing feedback on their work. Students who get nervous when answering questions in class may benefit from having the opportunity to draft their answers on a computer first.

Being Smart

Intelligent people aren't the only ones who can be smart. You can tell someone is intelligent by their level of self-awareness, level of preparation, level of cleverness, level of promptness, level of personal cleanliness, level of knowledge of current events, level of charisma, and level of social adeptness. Being intelligent boils down to the sum of your entire persona, character, and actions. You should pay attention to your intuition if something just doesn't feel right. Heed the advice of your intuition when trying to draw profitable business opportunities, clients, and partners your way. Intelligent people are able to see the bigger picture. They have a broad perspective and can recognize opportunities where others can't. Learning without stopping, you can always take in new information. If you believe you already know everything there is to know about making it in life and business, you will not continue your quest for information. Intelligent people constantly push themselves to learn more. They have access to the most recent information and are always expanding their horizons in terms of what they know, can do, believe, and how think. Improve your professional and personal life by reading industry-related articles, magazines, blogs, and books. Intelligent people never blindly accept the word of others. They are not content to blindly follow the herd, even if it is comprised of experts in their field, and will instead question authority. They consistently probe for deeper meaning and ask perceptive questions in order to improve the effectiveness of organizational processes. Risk-taking is nothing new for explorers. Intelligent people enjoy dabbling with cutting-edge tools and concepts. They are willing to take chances that could result in failure, but they are able to turn those setbacks into successes. Success comes more easily to them because of their insatiable curiosity and willingness to try new things. Smart people know that life isn't all about them, even though most people around them do. They have an incredible sense of humor and are able to laugh at themselves, find the good in bad situations, and look for the silver lining in the darkest clouds. Intelligent thought allows one to learn new things quickly and easily, apply that knowledge in ways that benefit others, and make sense of the world.

Effective Communication

From the moment we wake up and turn on the radio or newspaper to the time we reach the office and hear the train announcements or see an advertisement board on the way, we are constantly exposed to various forms of communication. The ability to effectively communicate with one another throughout the day helps us get more done and makes us and the company look more professional to clients and coworkers alike. Effective communication is a crucial skill in the business world. A common source of productivity problems is leaders who are unable to effectively convey their vision and goals to their teams. As we go about our daily lives, communication facilitates our social interactions by facilitating the exchange of information and the development of empathy. What makes life worth living is the capability to communicate our thoughts and feelings with others. It is vital that we share information with one another. Our ability to convey meaning through actions as well as words is crucial. In both our private and qualified lives, we rely on non-verbal cues like signals, body language, and facial expressions to convey meaning. Humans communicate through physical contact, including handshakes, eye contact, and touch. In fact, I'd argue that there are contexts in which non-verbal cues are more effective than words alone. Constantly make it easy for the receiver to grasp the point of your communication. Keeping your message brief will help ensure that it is received and understood. Short, direct messages that convey the intended meaning are preferred. Do not leave it up to conjecture for them to understand your message. If your message isn't crystal clear, the listener or reader won't be able to grasp its meaning and respond appropriately. When knowledge is lacking, assumptions are made. Evidence or facts are lacking, and it is easy to form assumptions if the right questions aren't posed. To get started, categorize your first thoughts as true or false. Asking more queries decreases the likelihood of making sweeping assumptions. To listen to another person with empathy means to pay close attention and react appropriately during a conversation. When you listen with empathy, you create a bond with the other person, which allows you to give a more genuine, specific response. Acquire an in-depth comprehension of their feelings and worldview. One must think carefully about what they will say before they say it, as their tone and word choice reveal much about who they are. Planning, preparation, and the formulation of what you want to say and achieve in the conversation in advance are all necessary for successful outcomes.

Having Exceptional Integrity

True strength lies in being honest. Maintaining your integrity and moral compass in the face of external pressures to conform can be challenging. It can be difficult to stay authentic in today's society. If you lacked moral rectitude, you would compromise your core values every time you bowed to social pressure. If you want to be considered a person of integrity, you must act in accordance with your principles. You tell people exactly who you are and what you believe in, regardless of whether or not they share your values. To be a person of integrity, you must remain true to yourself and never change to please others. You are who you are, owing to your integrity, and you know that losing either is never a good idea. In addition, those around you are more likely to trust your word because of your refreshingly forthright nature. People seek you out because you are unafraid to express your opinions and beliefs. Because of this, honesty is highly valued in a leader.

People put more faith and confidence in you when they know you have their best interests at heart. It's simple to have faith in someone who sticks to their principles, whether in business or personal relationships. Those who know you to be trustworthy will take what you say seriously. Having integrity makes you a better person in general, increasing your chances of success. With integrity, you are free to be yourself without altering your behavior to win the favor or applause of others. If people suspect you lack integrity, they might not put much stock in your word. You have a decent standing that will help your image because people find you to be reliable and trustworthy. People who are morally upright convey a positive image of themselves. To give up your values in order to fit in is a never-ending and exhausting struggle. Being honest about one's identity from the get-go is preferable to the stress of hiding who one really is. This is a load you shouldn't have to bear if you're an honest person, as it will cause you undue stress and anger. Having integrity gives you a strong sense of self-worth. Since a person lacking integrity is not being truthful about their morals and values, they have nothing to feel good about themselves. You can only exude confidence if you are at peace with yourself and allow that serenity to shine through in your interactions with others. When you act with honesty and morality, others will naturally be drawn to you. Just being honest and trustworthy will earn you respect from those around you. Since you probably don't want to hang out with a liar, it stands to reason that when you act with honesty and morality, you attract similarly honest and moral people into your life. It's natural to worry when you're being dishonest, and that can keep you up at night. When you're a person of high moral standards and unwavering honesty, you're able to drift off to dreamland without compromising your moral compass or affecting your level of awareness. Honesty isn't just the correct thing to do; it's also a source of serenity and calm. It has been communicated a lot about how important it is to have integrity, and that's absolutely true. Something should be said about a person who, despite the world's best efforts to convince them otherwise, chooses to live in accordance with their own set of moral and ethical principles. Having integrity is a commendable quality because it reveals the genuine you. Having the right morals is essential for inspiring and leading others, and we've already discussed how imperative it is for a leader to have integrity. Not being yourself is fatal to your leadership abilities. When mentoring, it's crucial to be trustworthy because your mentees will put all their faith in you. Those around you will be motivated to better themselves if you are an example of integrity. They will aspire to be just like you once they observe your honesty and strength of character.

Being Honest

Sincerity and truthfulness are essential components of honesty. To be truthful is to make it a lifelong habit. Honesty is a cornerstone of moral character, and it is a trait that can be found in people who practice it. An honest person is one who acts in a trustworthy manner at all times, never lies, never cheats, never gets late, and never takes advantage of others. When someone is honest, you can rely on them to tell you the truth. Honesty is a cornerstone of good character. Good character traits like compassion, self-control, forthrightness, and moral rectitude are fostered by an honest person. There is no place in Honesty for dishonest behaviors like lying, cheating, lack of trust, stealing, or greed. Sincere, trustworthy, and loyal people who are honest maintain these traits throughout their lives. Integrity is priceless, and it's the most crucial habit you can develop.

Honesty, first and foremost, encourages genuineness. Truthfulness conveys one's genuine emotions and ideas. Being truthful aids others in understanding who you truly are. Therefore, being truthful in one's expression is essential. If you're being truthful with yourself, you won't be afraid of anything. It boosts one's self-assurance and bravery. Having a lot of guts to tell the truth is essential. The courage, to tell the truth sets you apart. He or she who lies is a coward. Lying is an indication of insecurity. Honesty also helps you mature, which is a huge plus. Being truthful is a sign of maturity, without a doubt. If a person consistently tells the truth, that's a good sign that they're an adult. In addition, a person of maturity can deliver truthful feedback without causing offense. Relationships benefit greatly from being honest with one another. Having this common ground is a great help in fostering community. Most importantly, it encourages interpersonal interaction. The tranquility that comes with being trustworthy is a major perk of being truthful. The truth sets one free in every sense of the word. Truthful people like floating on air. This is due to the fact that he does not experience the mental and emotional burden of lying. Another benefit of honesty is that it eliminates the need for one to keep secrets. This whole situation is incredibly soothing. A person's credibility improves when they are honest. A person who is honest is held in the highest esteem. A person like that seems to have widespread support and admiration. In addition, people are more likely to feel comfortable opening up to a trustworthy individual. True honesty has been proven to prevent problems in one's life. Lies have the potential to alleviate distress in the short term. Nonetheless, lying only leads to deeper and deeper legal trouble. It doesn't take much for one lie to spark a chain reaction of one hundred more. So, being honest right off the bat is essential. This translates to an absolute requirement for integrity in all situations. Honesty is the best policy for attracting like-minded companions. Friendships made by a trustworthy individual tend to last a lifetime. The friendship between these people will be close and solid.

Being Courageous

Confidence in one's own abilities is a necessary but not sufficient condition for exhibiting courage. And without it, how could we possibly get anything done? Courage is a commendable quality, especially when put to good use. Courage is the most essential character trait. Without it, no other virtue could be sustained. Courage is the foundation upon which kindness, generosity, honesty, forgiveness, and selflessness rest. The level of bravery we possess comes to characterize us as we develop. When we take risks, we grow and take on more responsibilities and opportunities. With so little bravery, all of these lose out. Courage is essential for achieving almost any goal in life. If you lack courage, you won't take risks, and you won't be able to pick yourself up after a setback. If you're eager to take the risk, you'll learn and develop rapidly. Having courage does not imply an absence of fear but rather the willingness to confront and conquer that fear. It takes bravery to test one's limits, gain knowledge, and venture into uncharted territories. In the procedure of doing so, however, we make all of our greatest discoveries. We who appreciate its worth will go to any lengths to protect it. Happiness is an inevitable result of the freedom that comes from having the guts to take risks.

Being Self-Aware

The capacity for self-awareness consists in paying attention to how one's own thoughts, feelings, and deeds conform to or deviate from one's own values. To be truly self-aware, you must be able to take an unbiased look in the mirror, control your feelings, act in accordance with your principles, and grasp others' perspectives with accuracy. Self-aware people are able to step back and assess their own motives, emotions, and mental processes. This is a rare ability because most of us interpret events based on how we feel. In order to assess their own progress and that of their teams, leaders must cultivate self-awareness. Realizing how we might be perceived by the public is the essence of public self-awareness. This awareness makes us more likely to behave in ways that are generally accepted by society. There are positive outcomes to this level of consciousness, but it can easily tip into narcissism. Those who score higher than average on this trait may worry excessively about the opinions of others. Self-awareness is the ability to observe and examine one's own feelings and thoughts in private. People who are in touch with their inner selves are introspective and curious about their own thoughts, feelings, and actions. When you're getting ready for a big consultation, for instance, you might find that you're tense. An example of private self-awareness would be to notice the physical sensations and correctly attribute them to your anxiety about the meeting. Our reluctance to share parts of ourselves stems from the precarious balance between self-awareness and self-consciousness. We create a facade that conceals our true selves. When we take the time to inspect our inner lives, we gain insight into our beliefs, emotions, motivations, and, ultimately, our strengths and weaknesses. We are self-aware enough to know when our actions affect other people. Those who take the time to learn about themselves tend to enjoy life more and build stronger bonds with others. They feel more self-assured in themselves and their social interactions, and they're happier in their jobs. When we take a look around, we can see ourselves as others see us. The ability to empathize with others who think differently is closely linked to self-awareness. Leaders who have an accurate picture of themselves are more likely to inspire confidence in their followers and gain their respect.

Having the ability to affect results depends on our level of self-awareness. As a result, we're able to make wiser choices in the future. This boosts our assurance, allowing us to express ourselves more specifically and consciously. Because of this, we can see things from different angles. It helps us let go of preconceived notions and prejudices. It aids in fostering stronger bonds between us. We gain more control over our feelings as a result. Less stress is a result. And, finally, it raises our levels of happiness.

Being Organized

When there are a lot of things contending for your attention, it can be challenging to maintain order. However, being well-organized has been shown to improve health, boost mood, and reduce stress. Being disorganized can cause serious problems. Depression and anxiety are two of the possible outcomes. Physical dangers can also arise from clutter, such as an increased risk of fire and the accumulation of allergens like dust and mold. Stress can be mitigated through proper organization. Although you may not realize it, clutter can negatively impact your health by raising your stress levels. It's not always obvious what constitutes clutter and what does not. Put in some time to sort through everything and decide what stays and what goes. The amount of time expended on cleaning can be cut in half if you declutter your home. Keeping your life in order has been shown to reduce levels of cortisol, the body's primary stress hormone. A more organized person sleeps better. You can devote more time to essentials like rest when you make organization a top priority. Having a plan in place for each day will help you avoid getting side-tracked and ensure that you get everything that needs to be done. At night, when sleep is most important, you can put everything else on hold and relax. Prioritizing sleep helps you relax and unwind, which is a welcome side effect of your stress reduction efforts. A group advocating for dietary health. Eating healthily throughout the week helps to plan out your meals in advance and prepare them in bulk. It's easier to stick to a healthy diet when meals and snacks are already prepared in advance. Workplace efficiency is enhanced by order. If you're feeling burned out and overawed at work, declutter your workspace; an unorganized office is a surefire recipe for stress and inefficiency. Work more efficiently and avoid interruptions by maintaining a neat and tidy office. Maintaining order can strengthen your bonds with others. When you're preoccupied with the mess around you, it's hard to concentrate on the people you love. This includes both the bodily and mental aspects of your life, as well as the connections you've made outside of the office. It doesn't matter if you're someone who's always been super organized or someone who could use some pointers on getting their act together. Today is the day to begin cleaning up and organizing your life. You can begin living a more organized life by first taking stock of your shortcomings and then making some simple but significant adjustments.

Empathy

Having empathy is having the capacity to feel and comprehend the feelings of another person. Empathy can be better grasped if we separate it from similar concepts. For instance, the capacity for empathy necessitates an awareness of one's own unique identity and the ability to differentiate between oneself and other people. It's distinct from mimicry and imitation in that regard. Additionally, empathy is distinct from the related concept of sympathy, which involves being moved by the plight of another and wanting to offer assistance. Having empathy allows us to put ourselves in the shoes of those around us and react appropriately to their experiences.

Thirst for Knowledge

Successful people typically have an insatiable thirst for knowledge. Most likely, this is one of the reasons for their initial success. Many people who have achieved great success, including entrepreneurs, have a voracious appetite for knowledge. Curiosity drives them to seek out new information and experiences. Someone who has reached mastery in their field should never assume they know everything there is to know about it. There's always something to learn, and sometimes the most unexpected people can teach us something. Having a degree is a sign that you have met the minimum requirements for your field, but that doesn't mean you can do the work without additional training or experience. Likewise, a lack of formal education is no guarantee that an individual will perform poorly on the job. Business success requires more than just a degree; it also requires common sense, negotiation skills, sales ability, and a general understanding of the business world. The act of learning itself should be celebrated. Your curiosity and desire to learn will keep you young if you live a life of wonder. Unless you go through life with blinders, you can not help but pick up new information and skills. Every day, in every situation, and with every person we interact with, we are presented with new learning opportunities. To refuse to engage with that and instead prefer to remain in your familiar surroundings is to stunt your development and severely restrict your options in life. Learning improves the quality of life. Success in any field requires an attitude that is always open to learning something new. If you're an elite manager, you will take this philosophy one step further and recognize you can learn a great deal from your staff while also teaching and mentoring them. It takes a strong leader to recognize something is to be gained from observing and gaining insight from those around them.

Any person who wants to cultivate and grow into a successful human being will unquestionably benefit from adopting these values and making them a part of their daily lives.

Effective Parenting Is the Root of All Ethics

Everyone wants to know the secret to the perfect parent-child bond. Every parent wants to raise well-behaved, morally upright children, and they have a better chance of doing so with the help of positive parenting techniques. It's not a simple task, though. Additionally, it's crucial to understand the parent-child relationship is a mutually beneficial partnership. Parents can help bridge the generation gap by taking the lead once they've learned the skills they need as good parents. When parents learn to balance enabling and restricting their children, rewarding and punishing good behavior, and discouraging bad behavior, their children will not become spoiled. This helps them learn how to be responsible parents. Distancing oneself from one's offspring is a common result of parental incompetence. A child and parents can be strengthened through mutual comprehension. Parenting is so crucial because of the protection it provides children from harmful factors like poverty and criminal peers and the mediation of harmful ones like abuse. Care prevents harm to the young. Supporting a person's emotional well-being is an integral part of providing care. Limits must be established and upheld in ever-expanding contexts to ensure the safety of children and others. Development is the process of helping children reach their full potential by giving them the best possible opportunities to do so. Parents should impart in their children to respect others, appreciate what they have, be honest, try their best, accept responsibility for their actions, learn from their mistakes, avoid making snap judgments, own up to their own shortcomings, prioritize their health, think before you speak, and prioritize time with loved ones. Parents should introduce to their children the ability to prepare simple meals, maintain personal hygiene, drive a car, do laundry, budget their money, be aware of their surroundings, clean up after themselves, manage their time effectively, read and comprehend complex texts, and make nutritious food choices. These lessons are essential for their development into fulfilled human beings.

Some Scriptures That I Believe I Guide Us Toward Proper Ethical Living

"Whoever loves discipline loves knowledge, but he who hates reproof is stupid." – Proverbs 12:1

Someone must teach you in for you to learn. You have to give up your free will and accept their control. You recognize their superior wisdom. You recognize and realize your lack of merit. Being humble is essential, but unfortunately, most people lack it. Only truly noble individuals will humbly submit to another's authority to learn. To develop a passion for learning, one must enjoy being instructed by others. The only way to learn is to admit you were wrong or you lacked in a way or two. You were wrong because you either didn't know the facts or were aware of them but chose to ignore them. You may have taught others incorrectly and now have to face the consequences of your actions. Most men will do anything to protect their reputation, so only truly noble souls can admit to having made a mistake or not knowing something. Adapting is the only way to learn new things. Altering one's behavior to make way for development is a humbling and challenging process. To effect change, one must be willing to admit error, break long-held habits, and justify one's new ways of behaving to those around them. The price of transformation is too great for most men, but it is within reach of those with noble and humble souls.

"Whoever walks in integrity walks securely, but he who makes his ways crooked will be found out." – Proverbs 10:9

Integrity and behavior matter more than anything else. They decide whether or not God will bless or curse you, whether or not you will achieve your goals in life, and whether or not others will learn of your existence. It's preferable to avoid public shame by achieving success in life. One who walks upright has impeccable moral fiber, acting per God's standards of righteous behavior. Rather than empty rhetoric, you're putting in the effort. This kind of person's action is appropriate to God's ideal of what is right and good. The promised benefits are His favor, material prosperity, and freedom from worry that your hypocrisy will expose. A weak person perverts his ways, doing what he thinks is right rather than what God says is right. God will curse him, he will fail, and his hypocrisy will be exposed because of the dishonest ways he has chosen to cover them up. Living a life in complete accordance with God's word guarantees a life of blessing and success. Maintaining a godly life-style gives a man unwavering self-assurance, and enjoying God's favor safeguards him against falling. One's perverse rebellion will be exposed to others if he chooses his way in the face of advice and guidance and then suffers the consequences.

"A wise son makes a glad father, but a foolish man despises his mother." — *Proverbs* 15:20

God will reward you for being a wise child, and your parents will be overjoyed. Your ability to make your parents happy decides your future success. To honor one's parents is to honor God, who ordained them to that role and expects you to show gratitude for all they've done. Furthermore, God hand-picked your particular parents. No matter what you think of them or wish you had, God chose the two parents He knew would be best for you out of the over 4 billion that exist on Earth.

"Pride goes before destruction, and a haughty spirit before stumbling." — *Proverbs* 16:18

We should take joy in the Lord, remain faithful to the truth, and avoid sin. Lucifer's terrible, destructive fall from heaven began with his arrogant desire to be like God, to reach the heights of the heavens, and establish his throne above the stars of God. Because of the arrogance in his heart, he was cast down from his position of honor as God's covering cherub. Pride is destructive, and a haughty spirit will cause us to fall. The noxious nature of pride, self-will, self-importance, or arrogance should never be minimized. May we heed the warnings against the wickedness and the devastation that comes from arrogance and follow the many wise words that lead us in the way of righteousness pleasing to the Lord.

The only way, in my opinion, to have a successful life both in this world and the next is to instill in one's self the values of good ethics, become a good parent, and follow the word of God. This, in my view, is the only way to achieve success in both realms.

Chapter 7
Education

"*Teach me knowledge and good judgment, for I trust your commands." – Psalm 119:66*

Education must come first to fulfill any of the other fundamental requirements. Having a solid education is necessary to have overall success in life. It has a significant bearing on the progress that human society is making. Every citizen will be well-versed in their respective fields if they take the lead of our most accomplished citizens and follow in their footsteps.

A solid education can open the door to various career and life paths. It is beneficial for expanding one's knowledge and acquiring the skills necessary to employ that knowledge in real-world settings effectively. Many different methods and formats are used in educational settings, which can vary greatly from one nation to the next.

Some people believe applying theory in the classroom is unnecessary, while others believe that both types of education are equally important. Learning new skills is one way for individuals to improve their chances of success in the future. Students gain from this opportunity because they develop the skills necessary to enter the workforce and raise their standard of living.

Education's value can be increased in several ways, one of which is by helping students gain a deeper comprehension of the world. Reading, writing, and arithmetic are the subjects that are emphasized the most throughout the educational process.

The bestowal of knowledge transforms not only an individual's life but also a group and perhaps an entire generation. It is a wonderful blessing that has enabled us to alter history by learning the origins of the things around us and the inner workings of how they function.

An inward journey involves discovering one's identity and growing into that person over time. The knowledge we acquire in class can be applied to many facets of our lives. In addition, if we didn't learn these things, our lives would be very different. One of the most important things that education can teach you is to find inspiration in the words of others and the experiences of people who came before you. In my view, this is one of the most important benefits of education.

It is generally accepted that there are two primary types of education; theoretical and practical. The books we read in schools and universities are our primary education source. You are receiving an education in the theoretical realm. When people gain knowledge through hands-on experience, they have gained what is referred to as practical education. Students should place a significant emphasis on both of these considerations. Because of the intense competition in today's job market, students must acquire marketable skills that will increase their chances of finding work after their education. It is essential to acquire a fundamental understanding of theory. Both are necessary for our continued existence, and we cannot afford to ignore them.

A solid education is necessary to fulfill the obligation of being a responsible and ideal member of society, a responsibility that cannot be met without education.

Education is the only way to ensure a person will live up to their responsibilities as a citizen. Education is, therefore, extremely important for the country as a whole. Because of this, tuition-free public university education is the norm in every region of the world. They and the students aren't responsible for paying the tuition. However, when you get to the graduate level of your education, things shift around. It instructs a person on the responsibilities and safeguards afforded to him as a citizen of the country. That is the correct procedure to follow to obtain citizenship in any country. A citizen who has received a good education is priceless to any country. As a result, the government supports citizens' participation in educational opportunities.

The foundation of this society is comprised of a sizable population. In today's society, there is a diverse collection of individuals to be found. Indeed, some of us successfully combine being responsible with being polite. Such people are extremely important in today's society.

Unfortuitously, some individuals are a threat to everyone else in the world. The societal divide originates in a significant education gap between the two groups. When a person tries to better himself through education, he develops into a responsible and valuable member of society and his family. For this reason, it should be a top priority to ensure every member of society has access to an education of sufficient caliber.

The pursuit of one's education ought to be the highest priority. Many advantages come along with having a strong understanding of a topic. The first advantage is to have the chance to further your education, which everyone places a high value on. It brings the living standards up. The perspectives of people and how they act have undergone significant changes recently. An educated person maintains composure and courtesy in almost any circumstance. They have established a fairly high standard in terms of mentality. In addition to this, they have got a significant capacity for self-reflection.

The progressions that have been made in science and technology can be attributed to the high number of educated people. People with good manners and education will always have a place in their hearts for nature and animals. They value the future of our planet the same way we do, and their concern for maintaining the environment is justified. They can defend themselves against numerous irrational beliefs. Someone who views their loved ones in this manner is likely to achieve success in their life. A successful career and a fulfilled life are attaining a well-rounded education. The power of education has the potential to shed light on one's life.

If a country prioritizes the education of its citizens, particularly its young people, it can only increase its chances of economic growth and development. Because of this, educational institutions should emphasize educating students in marketable, applicable skills such as coding and robotics. We firmly believe that all national issues can be resolved if we successfully enhance the educational system. The contemporary human being is completely submerged in the digital world, which presents him with learning and discovery opportunities. Each new day brings numerous exciting opportunities to learn new things and improve one's existing abilities. Literacy is necessary for individuals who wish to navigate the ever-quickening pace of the information age successfully. Because of this, everyone must attend college.

Education is the initial step toward acquiring knowledge. The possibility of rapidly and painlessly acquiring knowledge has significantly increased. Literate people have a lower risk of being misled because they can locate information pertinent to them, think critically, and effectively apply what they learn. It demonstrates why you shouldn't put too much stock in the opinions expressed by strangers on the internet.

For example, a literate parent will have an easier time raising their children than an illiterate parent. The education and the knowledge they have gained will be extremely beneficial to their children. They, among other things, guide them through their schooling by assisting them with particular assignments and laying the groundwork for their future careers. This not only gives the children the confidence to pursue their goals but also makes their parents proud. Above all else, students view their instructors and parents as reflections of themselves; they aspire to be just like them and to carry out tasks as effectively as they do. Students see their teachers and parents as reflections of themselves. When parents have a solid educational background, they are looked up to as examples by their children, and this is excellent news for society as a whole.

The theoretical knowledge people have acquired from the time they enrolled in elementary school until the time they started working is typically passed down from generation to generation through books. However, the most important thing for most people isn't what they can learn from books but rather what they can learn from their own experiences. If a person has never been exposed to anything outside of the classroom, they may not be equipped to handle the challenges they will face in their everyday lives, despite their academic success.

Learning is necessary because the amount of information we possess significantly affects the quality of our lives. It is essential to broaden both your knowledge and skill set if you wish to increase the depth of your conversations with other people. An employee who has invested the time and effort to obtain the necessary training before an unanticipated crisis at work may be an invaluable resource during the crisis.

When students graduate from college having acquired all of the necessary knowledge, they can proceed to better things. One can try to pique a student's interest in education by describing the numerous benefits of education. It is still ultimately up to the student to develop this interest. It is unrealistic to believe that it will only take one day to master a new skill.

A person who is successful in learning has the mentality of a learner and learns of their own free will. For example, to learn how to cram for a test in college, a student must first learn how to memorize all of the important information and facts on the test. Assume that your opportunity to learn has not passed with the completion of the test. If a student wants to get anything out of their education, they have to take in the information and remember it so they can use it in the future. Many different avenues are open to a person seeking to increase their level of knowledge. Your local library likely has a collection of books, periodicals, newspapers, and reference work such as encyclopedias, among other things—more knowledge results in the creation of more useful tools.

For one thing, books are an excellent resource for learning specific information. The theoretical books contain ideas and information that can be applied appropriately. Reading books is an excellent method for enhancing one's intelligence and improving one's academic performance and professional prospects.

There is a wealth of information that students can benefit from outside of what is taught in classrooms. Certain information cannot be conveyed to students in text and must be left out.

To summarize, education is gained not only from reading books but also from life experiences outside the traditional classroom setting. Reading is one of the best ways to expand one's mental capabilities. On the other hand, they can learn how to handle issues that arise in the real world through their experiences.

The world over recognizes and values the contribution that parents make to the growth and development of their offspring. Nevertheless, in this setting, grandparents are frequently disregarded, despite the significance of their roles. Children who still have living grandparents have an advantage academically over their peers who do not.

Numerous studies have demonstrated that grandchildren who live with their parents enjoy better physical and mental health than their peers who do not have this privilege. In addition to this, grandparents can devote additional time and attention to the child. A newlywed couple will face many obstacles during childrearing; however, grandparents can contribute significantly. They have a wealth of practical experience, the first and most important qualification.

Grandparents are a treasure trove of knowledge and insight because they've witnessed more of the world and lived through more history than their grandchildren. They can share the knowledge and insight they have gained from their own experiences with subsequent generations. These kinds of lessons can be passed down from one generation to the next.

Children who live with their grandparents tend to have a higher level of happiness is no longer just anecdotal evidence but rather a scientific fact. Additionally, this relationship benefits all parties involved, particularly because it lowers depressive symptoms in the grandparents and the grandchildren. This is a significant advantage.

When a child is upset with their parents, their grandparents help them calm down and get over their frustration. Because it's in their nature to do so, grandparents are excellent at listening to their grandchildren whine and complain because they have the patience of saints. They can offer helpful direction to both children and their parents. People getting on in years have a deeper connection to their history and the stories it has to tell. Therefore, the child will have a connection to his ancestry if he has a close relationship with his grandparents. This is because grandparents are the child's biological parents.

In addition, if a person's ancestors achieved something noteworthy, they may encourage their descendants to do the same.

Grandparents have an incredible opportunity to instill in their grandchildren the importance of retaining a positive sense of humor in the face of adversity. Grandparents can form strong bonds of friendship with the grandchildren they are raising. It is only natural that adult males in today's society need to guard children. People of more advanced age are typically better able to show compassion and tolerance toward younger generations.

Grandparents have the potential to be exceptional role models for their grandchildren. They have more life experience and valuable lessons to impart to the younger generation than the older generation does. They can impart invaluable lessons on life to the younger generation. The generation that came before us had a significantly higher level of culture and was much more aware of social norms regarding appropriate attire. Unlike them, we enjoy relaxing in our casual wear. They will be able to instruct the child on proper attire in this way. They are available to lend a helping hand in an emergency.

In difficult times, it is extremely beneficial to have people you can lean on for support. Divorce and the loss of a parent are two of the most difficult life experiences a child can go through. In this situation, the grandparents are the primary caregivers for the children, and they go to great lengths to ensure that the children are protected. The most cherished members of any family are the grandchildren's grandparents. Put another way; they have the resources to provide a child with anything and everything that he might require. If you choose to entrust them with your child, you can have peace of mind knowing they will provide excellent care for your child. They comply with every demand that the child makes of them. They have a good time with them, they look after them, and they teach them new things. Because of their personal experiences with time, older people tend to have a higher appreciation for its passing. Therefore, they are now in a position to instill a value for time in their grandchildren by demonstrating the significance of their own time, mainly because there is always something new to try.

Grandparents can learn about the newest technology and fashion trends from their grandchildren, making them a valuable source of information. This interaction can go in either direction. Because of this, there is a possibility for increased learning. They love without attaching any conditions or prerequisites to it. The joy and pride they take in raising their grandchildren far outweigh the joy and pride they take in anything else they own. The influence of our grandparents has been consistently significant throughout our lives. They shower us with the unending and undivided love that they have. We should show them the respect they deserve before it's too late and it becomes impossible. It brings happiness to both of us, as well as to them.

It is important to gain education from all avenues of life, including parents, grandparents, friends, teachers, and especially the Bible.

A few scriptures that inspired me to pursue an education and instilled in me the value a proper education holds:

"The fear of the Lord is the beginning of knowledge, but fools despise wisdom and instruction." – Proverbs 1:7

"Day after day they pour forth speech; night after night they reveal knowledge." – Psalm 19:2

"The heart of the discerning acquires knowledge, for the ears of the wise seek it out." – Proverbs 18:15

"My child, listen to what I say, and treasure my commands. Tune your ears to wisdom, and concentrate on understanding." – Proverbs 2:1-2

"The Spirit of the Lord will rest on him— the Spirit of wisdom and of understanding, the Spirit of counsel and of might, the Spirit of the knowledge and fear of the Lord." — Isaiah 11:2

"Gold there is, and rubies in abundance, but lips that speak knowledge are a rare jewel." – Proverbs 20:15

Chapter 8
Helping Others

 arry each other's burdens, and so you will fulfill the law of Christ." – Galatians 6:2

It doesn't matter where you go; you'll find poor people. Even in the richest countries, the poorest citizens frequently have no choice but to make do with housing that does not meet basic requirements and to forego necessities such as heat, transportation, and nourishing food. Those economically disadvantaged typically also have a much lower quality of life in other aspects of their lives. The effects of poverty on young people can be devastating and last a lifetime; this is especially true in situations where they do not have access to adequate educational opportunities.

People who are struggling to make ends meet may choose to forego furthering their education to support themselves. As a result, they may lack the fundamental literacy and numeracy skills necessary to progress in their chosen careers. After a number of years have passed, their children are now in a very similar situation; their family has a low income, and there are few opportunities available to them other than to forego formal education in favor of working.

In some countries, a smaller percentage of the budget is spent on public education, which results in lower quality education that is both more difficult to obtain, especially for the poor and less accessible. There are several signs that a school district's budget is inadequate to meet the requirements to provide students with a quality education. These signs include overcrowding, broken furniture, and a lack of technology. Most educators either lack the necessary experience or training to instruct a specific topic or become uninterested in doing so. Due to these factors, children from low-income families are at a significant disadvantage.

Regarding the importance of education for developing nations, the subject can never receive enough attention. The classroom holds the answer to how individuals, families, and entire communities can break the cycle of poverty and lift themselves out of its grip for good. Education benefits future generations because it instills hope in children for a better world and the confidence to work toward realizing those hopes in the world around them.

Education is also of great value to adults, particularly in nutrition, health-care, and gender equality, which are relevant to their day-to-day lives and affect them directly. The pursuit of knowledge can be encouraged in the next generation by adults showing the way.

People who educate themselves about farming practices and agriculture acquire the knowledge that equips them with the tools necessary to culti-vate and uphold healthy crops, providing them with food and a source of income. Families also gain an understanding of the foods that pregnant women should eat to support the development of their babies, as well as the nutrients that their children require for healthy growth as a result of this education. In developing countries, the rapid spread of illness is frequently caused partly by a general lack of public knowledge regarding the mechanisms by which diseases are spread. In recent years, youth groups across the world assisted in spreading information about viruses and the importance of avoiding traditional burial practices that could potentially spread the virus to other people. Communities are receptive to new information, particularly when it is communicated by locals who are respected and whose opinions are valued. Education about the prevention of disease is essential at all times, not just during times of emergency.

Women need to have access to basic literacy skills because they need to be able to read about health information. As a direct consequence of this, the health of new mothers and their infants gets better, and fewer infant deaths occur during pregnancy. Literacy is also important in educating communities about clean water and sanitation because if families need to use sieves or boil water before drinking it to avoid waterborne illnesses, then educating communities about clean water and sanitation is important. Reading is beneficial to one's health in a variety of different ways.

Through participation in a variety of educational opportunities, it is possible to break the cycle of poverty. Education for girls, for instance, has been shown to lower the number of maternal deaths. This effect can have repercussions in areas of society that may, at first glance, appear to be unrelated. We know that education leads to improved decision-making regarding one's own health, as well as the health of one's children, one's career, and one's way of life. Even though many factors are involved in the connection between poverty and schooling, we know that education leads to improved decision-making.

Education is one of the most important factors in the fight for children's rights because it teaches both children and adults about the implication of respecting one another's parental roles regarding one's offspring.

One of the most well-organized ways to assist the needy and the disadvantaged is by providing them with a hand-up rather than a handout. When they are shown compassion through words of encouragement and genuine displays of humility and respect, they will know that someone cares about them and is genuinely trying to help them. They will know someone cares about them and is genuinely trying to help them. They would have more self-assurance and be better equipped to deal with daily challenges if they had access to opportunities for self-improvement that were available to them. Help those in need by directing them toward their capabilities and encouraging them to use those capabilities in appropriate contexts. Lend a helping hand to them, and show them that the resources they already possess are valuable enough that they can be used to meet their most basic requirements.

Social media platforms are rapidly becoming one of the most widespread and arguably easiest ways to provide assistance to the underprivileged around the world. By using social media and social networking sites, a person can connect with various charitable organizations or community centers that are engaged in assisting the needy. Additionally, a person can purchase goods online from websites that donate a portion of their proceeds to charities that assist the poor and needy. Participating in charitable events or joining an organization that provides aid to those in need are great ways to become a member of a community devoted to assisting those less fortunate. They can take part in a wide variety of events and organize a wide variety of strategies for fundraising, such as assisting with public awareness-raising campaigns, hosting a variety of shows, and other similar activities. They can take control of an organization and make significant contributions to its mission either as a member of its board of directors or its membership. One way to raise money is by accepting unrequited donations and auctioning those donations. To put it another way, this would be to raise the amount of revenue.

Feed those who are starving and those who are in need with nutritious food. Donations of food help those struggling to find a solution to their hunger problems. They are in such desperate straits that they cannot provide even a single meal for themselves or their families; the money you donate will assist them in obtaining food so they can maintain their health. It is better to donate food to someone who needs it rather than waste it or throw it away. Volunteering can be extremely rewarding, especially when it involves using one's time and skills to assist those struggling. Educating the general community about the significance of assisting the needy and disadvantaged can motivate more people to get involved in the effort to help those in need. It is possible to organize groups to help those in need by supplying them with food, transportation, and other necessities. Groups can provide this type of assistance. Help and instruction are two of the services that can be provided by volunteers. These people can assist in establishing free medical clinics in which people from disadvantaged backgrounds can consult with medical professionals. It's the insignificant details that make the biggest impact. It is possible to make a significant difference in the lives of those struggling by dedicating even a little time and effort each week. If the motivation is purely altruistic, it is possible to enlist the help of friends and family.

The organization of drives to collect essentials such as food, clothing, books, and blankets is one way to assist those impoverished and in need. Donation drives can be organized in any community, including schools, workplaces, and residential areas. The aid gathered during these drives will be distributed to those who need assistance. It is a straightforward approach to helping those in need. You should get in touch with organizations that help the poor to find out what supplies they require. Then you should organize a collection drive by putting containers at schools or other local premises where people can drop off their donations, and you should ask offices to donate to the drive. Develop some compassion for the difficulties faced by those who are less fortunate. Assist those you care about in overcoming adversity. To assist the needy and the poor, one must first be able to empathize with their wants, desires, and thoughts without degrading them, and then they must be assisted in a manner that is respectful for them to obtain those wants. Those in need should be shown compassion, and they should be treated with dignity. The effect on their day-to-day activities would be significant. Handle them in the same method as you would your closest friends and members of your own family. They would appreciate a positive response from you, such as a smile and some encouraging words. Donating unused goods, which can include anything from clothing and electronics to furniture and other items, is one way that people who want to help those less fortunate and less fortunate can do so. Make those in need the beneficiaries of your unused or unwanted items by donating them. It is a good deed that can make a difference to sort through one's old possessions to locate donations that can be given to people in need. Donations of warm clothing are extremely helpful to low-income and homeless people, especially during the year's colder months. Giving away unwanted items to charity can brighten the day of another person.

The process of recycling involves taking used materials and breaking them down into their parts so that those parts can then be reused for something else. This process was developed to recycle non-biodegradable materials such as plastics and metals. Since people have become more conscious of the effects of pollution and climate change, recycling has taken on an even superior level of significance.

Recycling is an important practice for a variety of reasons. Most importantly, it will assist us in our fight to save the planet. In addition, recycling helps save the environment by making it simpler to reprocess paper, which prevents the felling of millions of additional trees. This helps save the planet. As a result of the luxury with which many recyclables can be converted back into virgin materials, recycling enables us to save significant energy. It also contributes to the conservation of a great deal of material. Recycling is an activity that can help reduce the amount of pollution in the world. When energy is conserved, emissions of greenhouse gases and oxides are cut down significantly. Factories cause the majority of pollution by releasing harmful gases into the atmosphere. The decomposition process for waste that has not been recycled can take many years. The goods that are recycled also have value in the market. The majority of the products that we offer for sale today are produced with the utilization of recycled materials. As a direct consequence of this, recycling is an economically sound practice. Before any recyclable materials can be put to another use, they must first go through refining and cleaning. In addition, this section will talk about the process of recycling a variety of materials, each of which requires a particular sequence of steps.

Paper is the material that has the highest global utilization rate. Paper is made by compounding water and wood pulp in a pulping machine. To facilitate the processing of the paper, the shreds of paper are first dissolved in water. After that, chemicals are used to create a filter that removes the ink and the grime. In addition, once the filtering process is complete, the paper will have the consistency of mush, referred to as pulp. This will be transformed into clean paper. The process begins with the metal being shredded into very small pieces, followed by the metal being melted down and then shaped into something new. Glass can easily be recycled; old shards are melted down, and the molten glass is used to make new products. In this case, the production method that is used for plastic is utilized instead. On the other hand, recycling plastic can be difficult because different types of plastic must be separated before they can be recycled. Because there is such a wide variety of plastics available, each has characteristics that make it desirable and undesirable.

Recycling is possible for nearly everything we have in our homes, including but not limited to paper, plastic, metal, and glass goods, as well as furniture, toys, artifacts, and vehicles. Additionally, pick recyclable products that are readily available in commercial outlets. Utilize products that make use of recycled materials whenever it is possible to do so. Additionally, recyclable materials must be placed in the container designated for their disposal by the relevant authorities. Recycling is one of the simplest things that individuals can do to preserve the environment. Despite appearances, this seemingly insignificant action will have significant repercussions in the long run. In addition, before we get rid of the trash, we need to look through it prudently to determine whether or not there is anything that can be recycled.

Following are some scriptures that have guided me towards helping others and caring about the poor and needy:

JOCELYN FAMILY'S RULES

"Therefore, my brothers and sisters, you whom I love and long for, my joy and crown, stand firm in the Lord in this way, dear friends! I plead with Euodia and I plead with Syntyche to be of the same mind in the Lord. Yes, and I ask you, my true companion, help these women since they have contended at my side in the cause of the gospel, along with Clement and the rest of my co-workers, whose names are in the book of life. Rejoice in the Lord always. I will say it again: Rejoice! Let your gentleness be evident to all. The Lord is near. Do not be anxious about anything, but in every situation, by prayer and petition, with thanksgiving, present your requests to God. And the peace of God, which transcends all understanding, will guard your hearts and your minds in Christ Jesus. Finally, brothers and sisters, whatever is true, whatever is noble, whatever is right, whatever is pure, whatever is lovely, whatever is admirable, if anything is excellent or praiseworthy, think about such things. Whatever you have learned or received or heard from me, or seen in me, put it into practice. And the God of peace will be with you. I rejoiced greatly in the Lord that at last you renewed your concern for me. Indeed, you were concerned, but you had no opportunity to show it. I am not saying this because I am in need, for I have learned to be content whatever the circumstances. I know what it is to be in need, and I know what it is to have plenty. I have learned the secret of being content in any and every situation, whether well fed or hungry, whether living in plenty or in want. I can do all this through him who gives me strength. Yet it was good of you to share in my troubles. Moreover, as you Philippians know, in the early days of your acquaintance with the gospel, when I set out from Macedonia, not one church shared with me in the matter of giving and receiving, except you only; for even when I was in Thessalonica, you sent me aid more than once when I was in need. Not that I desire your gifts; what I desire is that more be credited to your account. I have received full payment and have more than enough. I am amply supplied, now that I have received from Epaphroditus the gifts you sent. They are a fragrant offering, an acceptable sacrifice, pleasing to God. And my God will meet all your needs according to the riches of his glory in Christ Jesus. To our God and Father be glory for ever and ever. Amen. Greet all God's people in Christ Jesus.

The brothers and sisters who are with me send greetings. All God's people here send you greetings, especially those who belong to Caesar's household. The grace of the Lord Jesus Christ be with your spirit. Amen." – Philippians 4

"Therefore, I urge you, brothers, in view of God's mercy, to offer your bodies as living sacrifices, holy and pleasing to God--this is your spiritual act of worship. Do not conform any longer to the pattern of this world, but be transformed by the renewing of your mind. Then you will be able to test and approve what God's will is--his good, pleasing and perfect will. For by the grace given me I say to every one of you: Do not think of yourself more highly than you ought, but rather think of yourself with sober judgment, in accordance with the measure of faith God has given you. Just as each of us has one body with many members, and these members do not all have the same function, so in Christ we who are many form one body, and each member belongs to all the others. We have different gifts, according to the grace given us. If a man's gift is prophesying, let him use it in proportion to his faith. If it is serving, let him serve; if it is teaching, let him teach; if it is encouraging, let him encourage; if it is contributing to the needs of others, let him give generously; if it is leadership, let him govern diligently; if it is showing mercy, let him do it cheerfully. Love must be sincere. Hate what is evil; cling to what is good. Be devoted to one another in brotherly love. Honor one another above yourselves. Never be lacking in zeal, but keep your spiritual fervor, serving the Lord. Be joyful in hope, patient in affliction, faithful in prayer. Share with God's people who are in need. Practice hospitality. Bless those who persecute you; bless and do not curse. Rejoice with those who rejoice; mourn with those who mourn. Live in harmony with one another. Do not be proud, but be willing to associate with people of low position. Do not be conceited. Do not repay anyone evil for evil. Be careful to do what is right in the eyes of everybody. If it is possible, as far as it depends on you, live at peace with everyone. Do not take revenge, my friends, but leave room for God's wrath, for it is written: "It is mine to avenge; I will repay," says the Lord. On the contrary: "If your enemy is hungry, feed him; if he is thirsty, give him something to drink. In

doing this, you will heap burning coals on his head." Do not be overcome by evil, but overcome evil with good." – Romans 12

"Therefore, rid yourselves of all malice and all deceit, hypocrisy, envy, and slander of every kind. Like newborn babies, crave pure spiritual milk, so that by it you may grow up in your salvation, now that you have tasted that the Lord is good. As you come to him, the living Stone—rejected by humans but chosen by God and precious to him, you also, like living stones, are being built into a spiritual house to be a holy priesthood, offering spiritual sacrifices acceptable to God through Jesus Christ. For in Scripture, it says: "See, I lay a stone in Zion, a chosen and precious cornerstone, and the one who trusts in him will never be put to shame." Now to you who believe, this stone is precious. But to those who do not believe, "The stone the builders rejected has become the cornerstone," and, "A stone that causes people to stumble and a rock that makes them fall." They stumble because they disobey the message, which is also what they were destined for. But you are a chosen people, a royal priesthood, a holy nation, God's special possession, that you may declare the praises of him who called you out of darkness into his wonderful light. Once you were not a people, but now you are the people of God; once you had not received mercy, but now you have received mercy. Dear friends, I urge you, as foreigners and exiles, to abstain from sinful desires, which wage war against your soul. Live such good lives among the pagans that, though they accuse you of doing wrong, they may see your good deeds and glorify God on the day he visits us. Submit yourselves for the Lord's sake to every human authority: whether to the emperor, as the supreme authority, or to governors, who are sent by him to punish those who do wrong and to commend those who do right. For it is God's will that by doing good you should silence the ignorant talk of foolish people. Live as free people, but do not use your freedom as a cover-up for evil; live as God's slaves. Show proper respect to everyone, love the family of believers, fear God, honor the emperor. Slaves, in reverent fear of God submit yourselves to your masters, not only to those who are good and considerate, but also to those who are harsh. For it is commendable if someone bears up under the pain of unjust *suffering because they are conscious of God. But how is it to your credit if you receive a beating for doing wrong and endure it? But if you suffer for doing good and you endure it, this is commendable before God. To this you were called, because Christ suffered for you, leaving you an example, that you should follow in his steps. "He committed no sin, and no deceit was found in his mouth." When they hurled their insults at him, he did not retaliate; when he suffered, he made no threats. Instead, he entrusted himself to him who judges justly. "He himself bore our sins" in his body on the cross, so that we might die to sins and live for righteousness; "by his wounds you have been healed." For "you were like sheep going astray," but now you have returned to the Shepherd and Overseer of your souls." –* 1 Peter 2

Growing up, my father always helped me, pushed me toward the path of God, and taught me that a life best lived is a life spent helping others.

I hope I have conveyed God's appropiate message, and I implore that Jocelyne Family Rules will help you live a fulfilling life full of peace, happiness, and grace. Amen.

Chapter 9
Jocelyn Family's Rules

"*Do not conform to the pattern of this world, but be transformed by the renewing of your mind. Then you will be able to test and approve what God's will is—his good, pleasing and perfect will.*" — *Romans 12:2*

Jocelyn's family's rules are about helping you achieve and become the best version of yourself and becoming a successful and morally upright person. These rules will surely help you become a good person. Being a good person is not particularly challenging, but it is not something that happens by chance. Above all else, you need to desire to improve yourself as a person and act in a way that is consistent with the principles you hold dear. Altering one's course through life is something that can always be done. How you carry yourself and the choices you make will determine your reputation. The general public could perceive certain individuals as greedy, dangerous, or self-centered. Some people have the reputation of being dependable, helpful, and devoted friends to those around them. Your reputation will play a significant role in determining the opportunities that come your way and will open doors for you.

The results of our choices can have an impact that is felt for years, if not for the rest of our lives. In the following paragraphs, we will discuss the significance of maintaining a good reputation and carrying out actions that are consistent with morality. Kind and considerate people are typically easy to find. They are courteous and subservient to others. They don't do this to win favor with other people or to demonstrate how valuable they are; rather, they do it because they genuinely value and appreciate being respected as an individual. You do not need to adopt a stiff, prim demeanor to be courteous, nor do you need to avoid potentially awkward situations at all costs. It is more important to ensure that your behavior is suitable for the setting in which you are currently located.

When things aren't going well in a relationship, it can put an incredible amount of strain on a person and leave a lasting mark on their character. When things aren't going well in a relationship, it can also put an incredible amount of strain on both parties. Sometimes a good person will try to stay in a relationship for too long, even though it is obvious that the sparks between them have faded. This can be frustrating for both parties involved in the relationship. On the other hand, a good person will be honest in their relationships, carrying on with them when things are going well and terminating them when things aren't going well. When you're involved in a relationship that's unhealthy for you, it isn't easy to live up to your full potential. It would help if you never hid your real feelings and kept your word.

A good person does not necessarily need to enjoy the company of everyone, but they should at least be courteous to everyone they encounter. They see people not only as they are now but also as what they can develop into. If someone is willing to help others, even if it means giving up something as insignificant as their shirt, that person is good. A good person is aware that having material possessions and a lot of money is meaningless if they do not have other people with whom they can share them. You don't have to be a selfless person who gives everything away; you have to be willing to assist those in need whenever you are in a position to do so. It is not difficult to behave in a self-centered manner and put one's requirements first in one's priorities. However, morally upright individuals consider how the outcomes of their actions will affect the people in their immediate environment. They are aware that something beneficial to them might not be the best option for everyone else. They are conscious of the effects their decisions will have on other people, but at the same time, they can make decisions independently of the people they care about.

A good person is careful, conscientious, and always willing to go the extra mile to ensure success. Staying behind to help clean up after an event or devoting their time to making sure something is done right are examples of how a good person demonstrates the importance of seeing a task through to its completion. Polite conduct, such as waiting to eat until everyone else has finished their meals or holding open a door for another person, will never go out of style. Good people are aware of the gravity of their actions and never forget the significance of having proper manners.

It is entirely possible to be a wonderful person in general while at the same time treating the people who are closest to your heart in the worst way imaginable. Good person is pleasant both in their own home and when they are out in public, and they do not take their frustrations out on the people closest to them. Making an effort to develop one's potential and evolve into a more admirable person is a never-ending process. They have realized that their past achievements do not necessarily indicate their future success.

Verses That Helped Me Become Morally Upright:

"For God so loved the world, that he gave his Son, that whosoever believeth in him should not perish, but have everlasting life." —John 3:16

The love that God has for people will never end. It was he who was responsible for the development of our minds. We are his biological offspring. He takes a personal interest in every one of us, learning about and falling in love with Himself. God had foresight into the challenges and ambiguity that would be inherent in the existence of humans. He had prepared himself for the possibility that we would fall short of our goals and make mistakes. As a result, He sent His Son, known as Jesus Christ, to the planet Earth. Jesus Christ lived a life free from all defects and devoid of sin. He taught us about the gospel and set a good example for us to follow in our daily lives. He presented himself as a sacrifice to take the punishment that we deserved for our sins. He is the gracious Redeemer who saves and redeems those who come to him. During His ministry here on Earth, Jesus promulgated the message of salvation. He said that we must first repent of our sins and then undergo baptism in both water and the Holy Spirit to be saved. Only then will we be forgiven for our transgressions. They will release us from our obligations. Because of what Jesus did, we can now accomplish this goal. Everyone who has lived will be resurrected to experience life again after dying. God has promised us that we can spend eternity in heaven with Him if we show our love for Him, believe in Him, and obediently follow the gospel that Jesus Christ has given us. God loves us and desires to see us happy both now and in the future is the primary reason He is so concerned with our well-being.

"Surely, he took up our pain and bore our suffering, yet we considered him punished by God, stricken by him, and afflicted. But he was pierced for our transgressions, he was crushed for our iniquities; the punishment that brought us peace was on him, and by his wounds, we are healed." – Isaiah 53:4-5

These verses explain not only the function of Christ's trial but also its significance. Jesus Christ, our Lord, took the punishment that we deserved for our sins upon himself and died in our place. We are all guilty of sinning and falling short of the glorious standard that God has set. Every person who engages in sinning does so in various ways, each of which they consider their "one true love." We sinners have earned every drop of misery and catastrophe poured out on us in this life. By placing the responsibility for our sins on Christ, we can be spared the destruction that would otherwise occur as a direct result of our sins. The purpose of this sacrifice was to make amends for the wrongs that we had done.

There is no other way to find salvation than through this route. The crown of thorns placed upon Christ's head, the nails were driven into his hands and feet, and the spear that was thrust into his side were all consequences of the sins we committed. He was sentenced to die as a consequence of our crimes. He endured suffering to provide the Holy Spirit and God's grace, which are the things that satisfy our hearts and minds. We will be able to persevere through the smaller tests that life throws at us as long as we have learned to value everything more than we value the possibility of losing anything and as long as we continue to love the one who loved us first.

"And do not swear by your head, for you cannot make even one hair white or black." – Matthew 5:36

Jesus is referring to the solemn ceremony observed when religious Jews, particularly Pharisees, took an oath. It was a typical facet of the culture during that period. Jesus condemned it as an immoral practice because it involved deceiving other people. That is to say, people made all of these grandiose oaths, but the reality that they were trying to create was entirely fictitious. The oaths made use of powerful language to drive home their point. Neither of these things gave the impression that the person taking the oath had any influence over the commitments. The individuals who took the oath to give the impression they were more impressive than they were had no intention of keeping the pledges or commitments that they were purportedly affirming by swearing some oath. They did nothing but deceive other people. It is both foolish and sinful to take an oath that you are aware you cannot keep, and it is also foolish and sinful to take any other form of an oath to win a debate.

The Moral Code Needed to Live a Fulfilling Life:

- God's love surrounds you. The light of God enlightens you, and the power of God protects you. He is always with you, and His eyes are always upon you.

- Do not be afraid; only believe. Whatever the situation, Jesus hasn't said his last word yet.
- Never give up; keep moving forward.
- Learn to manage your stress.
- Remember to focus on what is best for you.
- Never fail to try more.
- Believe in yourself; you can do it.
- You can learn from your mistake.
- Your perseverance will help you succeed
- What you can do today, please don't put it off until tomorrow.
- Choose your friends carefully.
- God and family should be the most important to you.
- Love holds a family together and is a blessing from God.
- Try before giving up.
- Problems are not eternal; they always have a solution.
- Don't let anyone insult you, humiliate you or lower your esteem.
- Listen before discussing.
- Those who don't value what they have, complain about having lost it one day.
- Communications are important.
- Financial education is very important (assets and liabilities). Learn to manage your money.

Some Pearls of Moral Wisdom:

- Anger is self-destructive.
- Good things don't come easy; the lesson you need to learn is the importance of patience.
- Be wary of consuming alcohol, illegal drugs, tobacco, smoking, and consuming harmful substances.
- Take enough time to make a decision.

- Learning is a treasure that follows you everywhere.
- Complaining will not get anything done.
- Perseverance is key to success.
- Determination leads you to your goal.
- Tenacity always gets the job done.
- Courage is the difference between success and never trying.

God has blessed me with the wisdom to live a fulfilling life that makes him happy, and I believe I must help others make God happy as well, for it is God alone who can make our life full of his precious blessings.

Acknowledgments